THE TOFU COOKBOOK

THE TOFU COOKBOOK

■ RECIPES FOR TRADITIONAL AND MODERN COOKING ■

Junko Lampert

ANGUS
& ROBERTSON
PUBLISHERS

ANGUS & ROBERTSON PUBLISHERS

Unit 4, Eden Park, 31 Waterloo Road,
North Ryde, NSW, Australia 2113, and
16 Golden Square, London W1R 4BN,
United Kingdom

First published in the USA by
Chronicle Books in 1986
First published in Australia
by Angus & Robertson Publishers in 1987
First published in the United Kingdom
by Angus & Robertson in 1987

Copyright © 1983 by Shufunotomo Co. Ltd.

Published by arrangement with
Chronicle Books, USA

ISBN 0 207 15491 0

Printed in Japan

Preface

Tofu, which has been an important ingredient in Asian cooking for hundreds of years, is becoming popular in the Western world. Not only is it available now in Oriental food stores in the West, but health food stores and supermarkets have begun to carry it. Many people, aware of the high nutritional value of tofu, would like to cook with it but have been frustrated by a lack of recipes. This book attempts to fill the gap. In it you will find both traditional recipes from China, and Japan, and "modern" Western recipes—that is, recipes for tofu dishes with European flavors, prepared with European cooking techniques. Most, if not all, of the ingredients will be readily available to you; in addition, the glossary of Asian ingredients on page 94 suggests appropriate substitutions.

Tofu is not only good for the health; it is also agreeable to the pocket book. But, perhaps most important, it can be prepared in many, many very tasty ways. As you use the recipes in this book and begin to see the possibilities for tofu in healthful, gourmet dishes, you may begin to invent recipes of your own. You may also wish to explore more fully the literature about tofu; in this case, let me recommend to you the remarkable encyclopedic work by William Shurtleff and Akiko Aoyagi, *The Book of Tofu*, published by Autumn Press, Inc.

I wish to express my gratitude to Mrs. Michiko Kinoshita of Shufunotomo, Co., Ltd., for her active support and excellent advice, and to Mrs. Laura Oberdorfer who transformed my halting English into a smooth text.

CONTENTS

                    Each recipe is 4 servings.

What is tofu?

Tofu, which is translated into English as "bean curd" or "soybean curd," is an important product of soybeans. We know that it was being used in China more than 2000 years ago and that it was introduced to Japan in a very early period of her history.

Tofu is rich in proteins, vitamins, and minerals. It is low in calories and saturated fats, and is entirely free of cholesterol. It is ready to eat when purchased, or it can be cooked further, as the recipes in this book will show.

From the Book of "TOFU HYAKU-CHIN" in 1782.

The different kinds of Japanese tofu

There are two kinds of white tofu: *momengoshi* and *kinugoshi*. *Momengoshi* (or "cotton" tofu) is a firm tofu and is the kind normally found in most stores in the west. *Kinugoshi* (or "silk tofu") is softer and smoother in texture than *momengoshi* and contains more whey. The most popular way of enjoying *kinugoshi* is in "*Hiyayakko*," an uncooked and chilled dish for hot summer days.

Yaki-dofu contains less liquid than *momengoshi* and is therefore more compact. It is cut into smaller pieces than the usual cake of tofu. *Yaki-dofu* has been grilled on both sides over charcoal, thus producing its firm texture; consequently, it maintains its shape well in boiled dishes such as *sukiyaki*. *Yaki-dofu* is generally available in cans in the West or can easily be prepared from *momengoshi*.

Whereas *yaki-dofu* is grilled, *agé* or *aburagé* is deep-fried. One-half inches (12 mm) slices of *momengoshi* are placed under a heavy weight for an hour or so in order to expel the liquid; after this, they are deep-fried twice until golden brown in color and chewy-crisp in texture. *Agé* is hollow in the center; you can slit open one side to form a pouch for stuffing, or you can slit it on three sides to make a flat sheet in which to wrap or roll other ingredients.

Nama-agé or *atsu-agé* is a thicker piece of tofu fried in the same manner as *agé*. The outer crust has the same texture and aroma as *agé*, but the inside is soft. *Nama-agé* is well suited for grilled or sautéed dishes.

Koya-dofu is freeze-dried tofu. It is named after Koya-san, a mountain whose summit is covered with Buddhist monasteries. Centuries ago the Buddhist monks there developed this method of treating tofu so that it could be preserved for several months. *Koya-dofu*, available in small air-tight packages, must be reconstituted before using. It absorbs liquid like a sponge, a characteristic which makes it ideal for cooking in a generous amount of well-flavored liquid.

Yuba is made from the skin which forms on the surface of soymilk when it is heated uncovered. It is sold in dried form in flat sheets, rolls, and sticks. *Yuba* is reconstituted by soaking it in warm water for a minute, then wrapping it in a damp towel and letting it stand for about 5 minutes until it becomes soft and pliable. Because *yuba* will fall apart if it is cooked too long, add it to the dish just before serving.

yuba

nama-agé or *atsu-agé*

Koya-dofu

gammodoki

okara

agé or *aburagé*

yaki-dofu

tofu: *momengoshi*

How to Prepare Tofu at Home

Ingredients:
For about 1½ pounds (675g) of tofu, you will need 2 cups of dried soybeans, a teaspoon of *nigari*, and water. *Nigari* is a solidifier or coagulator which is available in many health food stores and Japanese or Chinese grocery stores. You can also use Epsom salts or any acidic juice such as lemon or lime.

Method:
1. Wash soybeans thoroughly. Soak in 6 cups of water at least 8 hours in the summer and 12 hours in the winter.
2. Rinse and drain soybeans. Place ¼ or ⅕ of the soybeans into a blender, add an equal amount of water, and blend on high speed for about 3 minutes until it is smooth. This purée is called *go* or *go-jiru*. Blend the rest of the soybeans in the same way.
3. Bring 8 cups of water to a boil in a large pot. Pour in the *go* and bring back to a boil. Reduce heat to medium and cook, constantly stirring the bottom of the pot with a wooden spoon to prevent sticking. When the foam rises, turn off the heat.
4. Have ready a colander lined with a loosely woven tea towel or several layers of cheesecloth. Pour the *go* through the colander into another pot. Close the ends of the cloth and press gently to expel as much soymilk as possible. The fiber-rich material remaining in the cloth is called *okara*; empty it into a container for later use.
5. Bring the soymilk to a boil, and continue to boil over low heat for 5 minutes. Remove from the stove and let cool for about 5 minutes. Dissolve 1 teaspoon of *nigari* in 1 cup of water, and slowly stir it into the soymilk. Stop pouring in the *nigari* solution as soon as the soymilk begins to separate into fluffy cloud-like curds and a clear, pale yellow liquid (whey). Let the pot sit for about 10 minutes while the curds settle to the bottom.
6. Line a colander, or a container which has holes on the bottom, with a large cotton cloth. Slowly ladle the contents of the pot into the colander, and let it sit until no more whey drips out. Fold the ends of the cloth tightly over the curds, place a plate on top of it, and set a 1- or 2-pound (500 g ∼ 1 kg) weight on the plate. Let sit for 10–20 minutes. The heavier the weight and the longer it sits, the firmer the tofu will be.
7. When the tofu is firm enough, unwrap it and place it in a container with cold water to cover. Store in the refrigerator. See "Storing and Handling Tofu" for additional information.

Storing and Handling Tofu

Because tofu is often eaten uncooked or only briefly cooked, it should always be very fresh. Try to use it on the day of purchase. However, if you need to keep it for a few days, refrigerate it in a container deep enough so that you can cover it completely with cold water; change the water every day. Cover the container so that no food odors are absorbed by the tofu. Treated this way, tofu should remain fresh enough to use for about one week from the date it was made. This date is often printed on the container in which you purchased it. An added precaution which you can take after the tofu is a few days old is to boil it in water to which a pinch of salt has been added. Drain, rinse in cold water, and store as above. In addition to increasing the life of the tofu, salt will prevent it from becoming hard and porous when cooked. However, it will change the taste slightly, so use it only when necessary.

Care must be taken when removing a cake of tofu from the refrigerator container, for it breaks apart easily. One way to avoid this problem is to invert the container into a large bowl filled with water. The tofu will float and can be scooped up with your hand.

How to make *yuba* at home:

To make *yuba* you need thick soymilk. Follow the first 4 steps for preparing homemade tofu on page 10, except in step 3 reduce the amount of the water to 4 cups.

Pour soymilk into a heat-proof tray which will fit into a flat pan slightly larger than the tray. Pour hot water into the pan about half way to the height of the tray. Keep the water simmering over low heat. In about 7 minutes the surface of the soymilk will be covered by a yellow skin, *yuba*. Slide a bamboo stick under one edge of the *yuba*, roll it slightly to let *yuba* stick around it. Then lift *yuba* gently off soymilk and spread over a bamboo mat.

Preparatory Techniques

How to cut tofu

1. **Diced**

   Cut tofu into ½ inch (12 mm) cubes. This is the most popular cut for *miso* soup.

2. **Rectangles**

   Cut the cake of tofu lengthwise into two pieces, then slice it crosswise at ½ inch (12 mm) intervals. This cut is used for *Dengaku, Mabo-dofu*, etc.

3. **Chrysanthemum cut**

   Cut a cake of tofu into quarters. Place the largest surface uppermost and cut it lengthwise and crosswise at ¼ inch (6 mm) intervals. Do not slice all the way down, but leave the bottom ½ inch (12 mm) uncut. One way to ensure that you do not cut too far is to place the tofu between several chopsticks which will act as guards. Place in a soup bowl and gently open the ends.

4. **Tofu balls**

   Use a melon ball cutter or small spoon to scoop out small balls of tofu for soup.

5. **Crumbled tofu**

   Place ¼ (6 mm) of a cake of tofu in the palm of your hand. Tighten your fingers around it, squeezing until the tofu crumbles. This is used for scrambled tofu dishes.

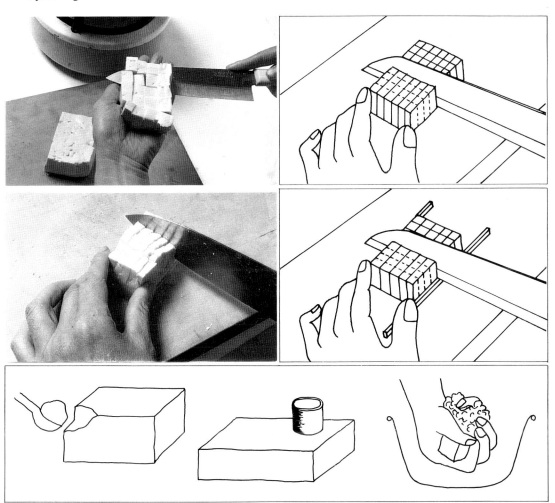

How to remove excess moisture from tofu

Regular Japanese tofu (*momengoshi*) contains almost 85% water. Depending upon what dish you are preparing, you will want to remove some of the moisture. The following procedures are listed in order, the first removing the smallest amount of water and the fourth removing the most.

1. **Draining**—when just a little water needs to be removed. Place a bamboo mat (*sudaré*) or folded towel on a plate. Set tofu on it and let it stand for 1 or 2 hours. For soup and *agédashi*.
2. **Pressing with a light weight**—when about ⅓ of the water needs to be removed. Wrap tofu in a dry towel and place on a cutting board. Raise one end of the board several inches. Put another cutting board on top of the tofu and let sit for 20 minutes. Used for *shira-aé*, scrambled dishes, and *dengaku*.
3. **Pressing with a heavier weight**—when 50% or more of the water needs to be removed. Follow the directions for pressing with a light weight; then place a 2-to-5-pound (1 ~ 2.5 kg) weight on top. Let sit for 20 minutes. Used for Chinese dishes.
4. **Squeezing**—Place tofu in boiling water; turn heat to low and cook for 5 minutes. Drain and put into a cotton sack; you can also use a large towel—gather up the ends to form a sack. Twist and squeeze the sack in order to expel as much water as possible.

Techniques used with *agé*

Removing excess oil: Plunge *agé* into boiling water and let sit for a minute or two; rinse immediately with cold water. Drain.

Opening up a pouch in *agé*: The *agé* will separate easier if you roll back and forth over the surface with a rolling pin. Make a slit on one side, insert both thumbs in the slit and gently pull apart. Do not use a jerking motion, but pull smoothly.

How to reconstitute *koya-dofu* (freeze-dried tofu)

When you first open the air-tight package containing *koya-dofu*, you will be struck by the smell of ammonia. Ammonia gas is added to *koya-dofu* because it makes the tofu become soft and absorbent and swell to double its original size during cooking. The process below will completely remove both the smell and taste of ammonia.

   Follow these instructions unless the package you have bought gives other directions.

1.   Use a bowl large enough to allow the *koya-dofu* to expand to double its size. Pour in a generous amount of hot water, and place *koya-dofu* in it. When one side is thoroughly wet, turn the *koya-dofu* over.
2.   Select a plate or lid a little smaller than the rim of the bowl, place it over the *koya-dofu* so that it weights the tofu down slightly. Let sit for several minutes. When the *koya-dofu* has doubled in size, cut one piece in half. If the center is still hard and white, let sit a little longer until it is soft all the way through.
3.   Pour off the hot water and replace with warm water. Press the *koya-dofu* between your palms, squeezing out the milky liquid. Repeat this process several times, changing the water as often as necessary until the liquid that you squeeze out is no longer milky. When the liquid is clear, you will know that all of the ammonia has been removed.
4.   To finish the process, squeeze out as much water as possible.

How to clean and prepare *okara* for cooking

Rich in fiber and protein, *okara* is a by-product of tofu making. In the West, it is generally not available in health food stores or supermarkets; however, you can obtain it by preparing your own tofu or by going to a tofu-maker's shop. Your own okara will be clean, of course, but that bought in a tofu shop should be carefully inspected for dirt particles. After picking out the dirt, place the *okara* in a sieve and set it in a bowl filled with water. Wash by shifting the sieve back and forth in the water or by stirring the *okara* with chopsticks. Drain, then place the *okara* in a cotton sack (or in the middle of a large towel whose ends you gather up to form a sack). Squeeze out the moisture. To obtain a finer texture, place the *okara* in a Japanese mortar (*suribachi*) and grind. An even smoother texture will be produced by pushing the *okara* through a sieve.

Utensils

There is very little special equipment needed for Oriental cooking. Occasionally, the recipes in this book will suggest that you use a utensil unknown in Western cooking, but you can usually improvise it with items at hand. Described below are the utensils most frequently mentioned in the recipes:

BAMBOO MAT (*Sudaré*):
Narrow strips of bamboo are held together by cotton string. Bamboo mats are used for shaping soft ingredients, draining and pressing out excess moisture. A flexible place mat could be used as a substitute; a kitchen towel can be used when expelling moisture is the object.

DROP LID (*Otoshi-buta*):
This is a lightweight wooden lid slightly smaller than the circumference of the cooking pot. In simmered dishes, it is placed directly on top of the ingredients to keep them immersed in the liquid, enabling the flavors to be absorbed. There are several good substitutes for *otoshi-buta*: a flat lid of a pot slightly smaller than the cooking pot, a heatproof plate, aluminum foil pie tin, or a circle of heavy-duty foil. If the pie tin is the same size as the pot, slash it in several places so that the steam can rise and the pie tin will remain directly on top of the ingredients.

GRATER (*Oroshi-gané*):
Japanese graters have two degrees of fineness, one for *daikon* (white radish) and a finer one for ginger. While the finest side of a 4-sided Western grater will do an adequate job for *daikon*, the Japanese grater should be used for ginger. *Oroshi-gané* are inexpensive and readily available in Oriental food stores, so this is one utensil that you might consider acquiring.

MORTAR & PESTLE (*Suribachi & Surikogi*):
The Japanese mortar is a pottery bowl serrated on the inside; it comes in various sizes. The pestle is of wood and also comes in various lengths; buy a fairly long one, for it is easier to work with. The hand mixers, blenders, and food processors with which your kitchen may already be equipped can be used in many of the recipes which ask you to grind the ingredients. Ground sesame seeds should be crunchy, with some of the seeds only half-crushed; a rolling pin can do the job adequately.

STEAMER:
Both bamboo and metal steamers are becoming increasingly popular and available in the West. Since they can be utilized in Western cooking (most simply, in preparing delicious, healthful vegetables), the purchase of this piece of equipment is worth considering. Steamers are also easy to improvise. You can use a cake cooler if it is small enough to fit the bottom of your saucepan. Or you can use several empty flat cans such as the ones tuna and salmon come in; cut off both ends of the cans. When steaming foods, it is important to begin with a steamer already full of steam: be sure to bring an inch (2.5 cm) of water to a full boil in the steamer before placing the food in it. Also, keep another pot of water boiling on the stove to add if during the cooking process the steamer runs dry.

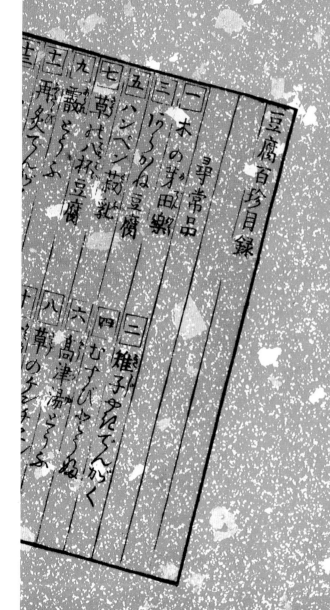

Recipes

Clear Soup with Tofu: 3 Variations

Dashi (clear soup stock)
4 cups *kombu-katsuo dashi*

Ingredients:
5 cups water
4 inches (10 cm) *kombu*
1 cup bonito flakes

Method:
Wipe *kombu* with a damp cloth. Place in a saucepan, cover with the water, and let soak for an hour. Place over high heat. Just before water comes to a boil, remove the *kombu*. Add bonito flakes, and bring back just to the boiling point. Reduce heat to low and simmer for a minute, skimming off as much foam as possible. Remove pan from stove and let sit until the bonito flakes have sunk to the bottom. Spoon off the clear liquid; be gentle so as not to stir up the bonito flakes at the bottom, for good *dashi* should be crystal clear. To ensure its clarity strain the skimmed *dashi* through a sieve lined with cheesecloth. Makes about 4 cups.

(1)
Ingredients:

2 cakes tofu (1 lb., 450 g)	Tofu seasonings:
5–10 string beans	1 egg yolk
4 cups *dashi*	1 teaspoon salt
4 strips of lemon peel or *yuzu*.	2 teaspoons sugar
Salt	1 tablespoon cornstarch
	2 tablespoons grated lemon peel

Method:
1. Press tofu between two cutting boards. Pat tofu dry, then place on a towel, draw up the ends, and crumble thoroughly. Place in a Japanese mortar (*suribachi*), along with the tofu seasonings, and mash until very smooth and well mixed. (You can also use a mixer for the preceding step.)
2. Wet a towel and wring it out thoroughly. Place the tofu mixture on the towel and shape into a cylinder, 2 inches (5 cm) in diameter. Wrap the towel firmly around the cylinder and tie the ends. Roll up in a bamboo mat (*sudaré*), and tie the mat in several places. Steam over high heat for 20 minutes. Cool thoroughly; then cut into ⅔-inch (1.5 cm) slices.
3. Cut the string beans into thin slivers, and parboil in lightly salted water.
4. Bring *dashi* to a boil. Warm the tofu one slice at a time by lowering it into the *dashi* in a slotted spoon. Divide tofu and string beans among 4 soup bowls, and pour in the *dashi* seasoned with a little salt. Garnish with a strip of lemon peel or *yuzu*.

(2)
Ingredients:

1 cake tofu (½ lb., 225 g)	1 ½ teaspoons salt
¼ lb. (120 g) mushrooms (*shimeji*, if available)	1 teaspoon soy sauce (*shoyu*)
4 cups *dashi*	4 strips of lemon peel

Method:
1. Drain tofu on a bamboo mat (*sudaré*) or folded towel. Clean mushrooms and cook in 2 cups of the *dashi* seasoned with salt and soy sauce. Remove mushrooms and keep warm. Add the rest of the *dashi* to the saucepan.

2. Cut the tofu into long strips and add to the *dashi*. Bring just to a boil. Add more salt, if needed. Divide tofu and mushrooms among 4 soup bowls. Gently pour in the *dashi* and garnish each bowl with the lemon peel.

(3)
Ingredients:

1 cake tofu (½ lb., 230 g)	1½ teaspoons salt
¼ lb. (120 g) spinach	1 teaspoon soy sauce (*shoyu*)
4 cups *dashi*	1 tablespoon fresh ginger, grated

Method:
1. Drain tofu on a bamboo mat (*sudaré*) or folded towel, then cut into 4 cubes. Make a "Chrysanthemum" from each cube. (See page 13.)
2. Parboil the spinach, then rinse immediately in cold water to stop the cooking. Drain and cut into 2-inch (5 cm) lengths.
3. Bring *dashi* to a boil, and season with salt and soy sauce. Using a wide spoon or spatula, carefully lower the tofu chrysanthemums into the *dashi*. Return just to a boil. Place tofu in 4 soup bowls. Check soup for seasoning, then pour gently over the tofu. Put a bit of grated ginger in the center of the tofu flowers. Place spinach beside tofu and serve immediately.

Miso Soup with Tofu: Basic Recipes and Variations

Ingredients:
4 cups *dashi*
Choice of vegetables or *wakamé* seaweed
4 tablespoons red *miso*, or 5 tablespoons white *miso*
Tofu (1 cake—about ½ lb., 230 g)
Garnish

Method:
Cook the vegetables in heated *dashi*. Soften *miso* in a small bowl by mixing it with a little hot *dashi*; then pour it into the saucepan. Bring to a boil, add the tofu, and return just to a boil. Pour into individual soup bowls, garnish, and serve immediately.

Variations:
(1) Cut 1 cake of tofu into ½-inch (1 cm) cubes. Rinse ¼ cup dried *wakamé*, soak in water to cover for 15 to 30 minutes; drain and cut into 1-inch (2.5 cm) pieces. Use red *miso* and garnish with chopped green onions.
(2) Cut 1 cake of tofu into ½-inch (1 cm) cubes. Drain ½ cup canned *naméko* mushrooms. Use red *miso* and garnish with chopped green onions.
(3) Cut 1 cake of tofu into ⅓-inch (8 mm) cubes. Cut *daikon* (white radish) into thin slices, 1-inch (3 cm) long, ½-inch (1 cm) wide. Cut 2 strips of bacon into ½-inch (1 cm) pieces. (You may use *agé* instead of bacon.) Use white *miso* and garnish with chopped chives.
(4) Cut 1 cake of tofu into ⅓-inch (8 mm) cubes. Cut 1 very small eggplant into ⅛-inch (3 mm) slices. Use a Japanese or Italian eggplant weighing about 4 oz. (120 g), if available. Use white *miso* and garnish with grated fresh ginger.

(1) (2)

(3) (4)

Tofu Cream Soup

Ingredients:
1 cup crumbled tofu
2 tablespoons butter
1 ½ tablespoons flour
1 ½ cups milk
2 bouillon cubes
½ teaspoon salt
Pepper
½ cup heavy cream
Chopped chives

Method:
1. Beat tofu in a blender until smooth.
2. Over low heat, melt butter in a heavy saucepan. Add flour, stirring it constantly with a wooden spoon and not allowing it to brown. Continuing to stir, gradually add milk.
3. Add the bouillon cubes, pressing them with the back of the spoon so that they crumble quickly and can be mixed into the soup.
4. After the bouillon cubes have dissolved, add the puréed tofu. Season with salt and pepper. Bring rapidly up to a boil, and remove immediately from the fire.
5. Stir in the cream. Serve sprinkled with chives.

Soup with Dried Cod and Pork

Ingredients:
7 oz. (200 g) dried, salted cod
⅓ lb. (150 g) pork, thinly sliced.
   Use pork belly, if available.
½ lb. (225 g) tofu
1 inch (2.5 cm) piece of fresh ginger root
5–6 cups soup stock
2 tablespoons *sake*
1 tablespoon sesame oil

Method:

1. Wash cod and soak in water overnight. If the cod is still too hard the next day, or if you have not had time to soak it overnight, steam it in the soaking water until soft. Cut it into bite-sized pieces. Reserve the soaking water.

2. Cut sliced bacon into 1 inch (2.5 cm) pieces.

3. Dice tofu into 1 inch (2.5 cm) cubes.

4. Peel ginger root and cut into very thin threads.

5. Combine soup stock with 1 cup of reserved soaking water. Bring to a boil. Add cod and pork, and bring back to a boil. Lower heat and simmer for ½ hour, skimming frequently.

6. Add *sake* and more salt, if necessary. However, be sure to taste the soup first because the cod may provide enough saltiness.

7. Add tofu and cook until the tofu rises to the surface.

8. Just before serving, add the ginger root and sprinkle with sesame oil.

Hiyayakko

A chilled tofu dish for hot summer days

Ingredients:
2 cakes tofu (1 lb., 450 g)
Garnishes:
   grated fresh ginger
   finely shredded green *shiso* leaves
   bonito flakes
   chopped green onions or chives
   thinly sliced *myoga* or celery
   1 sheet of *nori*, held briefly over flame to crisp, then crumbled
Soy sauce (*shoyu*), lemon juice

Method:
1. Boil tofu for a few seconds. Drain on a bamboo mat (*sudaré*). Cut each cake into 6 to 8 pieces, and place in a serving dish filled with ice water.
2. Put each of the garnishes into its own little serving dish.
3. Combine equal parts of soy sauce and lemon juice to make a dipping sauce.
4. Give each person a small saucer of dipping sauce. Lift the tofu out of the water with a slotted spoon, dip it into the lemon juice-soy sauce mixture and then into one of the garnishes. Use only one garnish per piece of tofu, but vary the garnishes from piece to piece so that you can experience a variety of flavors.

Appetizers: 5 Variations

Chilled Tofu

Ingredients:
1 lb. (450 g) tofu
1 tablespoon ginger juice*
3 tablespoons soy sauce (*shoyu*)
1 small cucumber
4–5 small chrysanthemum blossoms (optional)
Vinegar
1 tablespoon grated ginger

Method:
1. Place tofu in a pot, cover with water, and bring to a boil. Lower heat to medium and cook until tofu begins to sway. Drain and wrap tofu in a large cloth. Place between two heavy cutting boards and let stand for 15 minutes.
2. Combine ginger juice and soy sauce.
3. Pat tofu dry. Place on a heatproof dish and brush with the ginger-soy sauce mixtures. Place in a steamer* and steam over low heat for 12 or 13 minutes, brushing tofu with the sauce several times.
4. Remove from steamer. Let cool to room temperature, then refrigerate until thoroughly chilled.
5. Shred cucumber and place in cold water to crisp. Briefly cook chrysanthemum blossoms in boiling water to which a little vinegar has been added; drain and rinse with cold water. Press flowers and shredded cucumber between the palms to remove water.
6. To assemble dish, cut the tofu into ½-inch (1.5 cm) slices and arrange on plate. Decorate with the cucumber and flowers; place the grated ginger in a mound on the dish.

*Note:
See page 94 for ginger juice and page 16 for directions for steaming.

Sautéed *Agé* with Spinach

Ingredients:
1 lb. (450 g) spinach
2 pieces of *agé*, 2 × 4 inches (5 × 10 cm) each
2 tablespoons vegetable oil
3–5 tablespoons soy sauce (*shoyu*)
2 tablespoons *sake*

Method:
1. Wash spinach. Cut into pieces 2 inches (5 cm) long.
2. Boil *agé* briefly; drain and rinse with cold water. Cut into strips ¼ inch (6 mm) wide.
3. Heat vegetable oil in a frying pan; add spinach and cook for 3 minutes. Add *agé* and cook for another 3 minutes. Stir in the soy sauce and *sake*, and simmer for an additional 5 minutes.

Grilled *Atsu-agé*

Ingredients:

2 *atsu-agé*
1 tablespoon grated ginger
Soy sauce (*shoyu*)
½ cup shredded cucumber
grated rind of ½ lemon

Method:

1. Place the cakes of *atsu-agé* in a colander and pour hot water over them to remove excess oil. Pat dry with a towel.
2. Place in a preheated broiler and grill on both sides until deep golden brown.
3. To serve, cut each cake of *atsu-agé* into four slices, and divide among 4 plates. Top with a bit of grated ginger. Garnish with cucumber and lemon rind. Serve immediately with soy sauce, which each person pours over the *atsu-agé*.

Grilled *Agé* with *Miso* Filling

Ingredients:

4 *agé* (2 × 4 inches (5 × 10 cm) each)
4 teaspoons red *miso*
4 tablespoons minced spring onions or chives
1 teaspoon sugar
4 tablespoons grated *daikon* (giant white radish), or *momiji-oroshi* (see page 30 for directions)

Method:

1. Slit open one of the 4-inch (10 cm) edges of the *agé*, insert your thumbs and gently pull apart to make flat pouches with a wide opening.
2. Mix the *miso* with the spring onions and sugar. Spread a thin layer of the mixture over the inside of the pouches.
3. Grill both sides of the *agé* over charcoal or in a preheated oven broiler.
4. Cut in half crosswise, and serve immediately with 1 tablespoon of grated white radish on each plate.

Rolled *Agé*

Ingredients:

4 pieces of *agé*, 2 × 4 inches (5 × 10 cm) each
Miso
16 *shiso* leaves
4 tablespoons vegetable oil

Method:

1. Slit all four sides of the *agé* pieces and pull apart. Spread a very thin layer of *miso* over the white uncooked side of the *agé*. Place 2 *shiso* leaves on each piece of *agé*, and roll up tightly starting with the 4-inch (10 cm) end. Fasten with toothpicks.
2. Heat the oil in a frying pan, and fry the *agé* rolls over medium heat, turning them frequently so that they brown evenly.
3. To serve, remove the toothpicks and cut the rolls into 1-inch (2.5 cm) lengths. Japanese pickled vegetables are a good accompaniment.

Yudofu

A dish for cold winter nights, cooked right at the table in an earthenware casserole set on an electric burner or gas ring. A fondue pot or deep electric frying pan can also be used.

Ingredients:
4 cakes tofu (½ lb., 225 g each)
10 inches (25 cm) *kombu*
Dipping sauce:
   ¼ cup bonito flakes
   ¼ cup water
   ½ cup soy sauce (*shoyu*)
   1 tablespoon *mirin*
Garnishes:
   momiji-oroshi
   bonito flakes
   chopped green onions or chives
   1 sheet *nori* (seaweed)
   fresh ginger

Method:
1. Combine ingredients for the dipping sauce in a small saucepan and bring to a boil. Strain and pour into a small heatproof pitcher or mug.
2. Prepare the garnishes. For "red-maple radish" (*momiji-oroshi*), peel the white radish, and punch several holes in one end with a chopstick. Insert the red peppers in the holes, pushing them in with the chopstick. Grate them together. Also, chop the green onions; grate the fresh ginger; hold the *nori* very briefly over a flame to crisp, then crumble it. Serve each garnish in a separate bowl.
3. Wipe the *kombu* with a damp cloth, and cut several slits along each of the long edges with scissors to release the flavors during the simmering. Place in a casserole which should be ⅔ full of water. Put the pitcher of dipping sauce in the water. (A *yudofu* casserole has a special rack for the pitcher; if you are using an ordinary pot, place the pitcher in the center.)
4. Cut the tofu into 1-inch (2.5 cm) cubes or into slices measuring 2 × 2 × ⅓ inch (5 × 5 × 0.8 cm).
5. Bring the water to a boil. Slip some of the tofu into the water. The tofu is ready to eat when it begins to sway in the simmering water. Heat the tofu in several batches so that you do not overcook it.
6. Each guest pours or ladles dipping sauce into his own bowl and adds to it the garnishes of his choice. He serves himself some tofu from the pot and dips it into the sauce before eating.

Tarachiri (Table-Cooked Cod with Tofu)

Ingredients:
1 lb. (450 g) fresh cod
⅓ Chinese cabbage
20 stalks spinach
4 fresh or dried *shiitake*
¼ lb. (100 g) *enokidake* mushrooms, if available
1 cake tofu (½ lb. 225 g)
Dashikobu, 6 × 6 inches (15 × 15 cm)
Serving condiments:
  momiji-oroshi (see page 30 for directions)
  soy sauce (*shoyu*)
  lemon juice
  minced green onion

Method:
1. Cut the cod into bite-sized pieces, parboil in salted water, and wash off blood and scales.
2. Parboil Chinese cabbage, rinse with cold water and squeeze out liquid. Using the same hot water, parboil spinach, rinse thoroughly with cold water and remove moisture in the same way. Spread Chinese cabbage on a bamboo mat (*sudaré*), place spinach along the center and roll firmly. Cut in 2-inch (5 cm) pieces. Cut off the stems of the *shiitake* and discard. Make decorative cuts on the surface of the cap. If dried *shiitake* are used, soak them in warm water for 20 minutes in advance and proceed as above.
3. Cut off half of the stems of the *enokidake* and discard. Wash quickly with cold water and drain well.
4. Cut tofu in 1-inch cubes. Arrange all the ingredients on a large plate.
5. Wipe the *dashikobu* with a wet cloth, spread it on the bottom of an earthen pot. Pour in water and bring to a boil.
6. Pull out the *dashikobu* and put the other ingredients into the boiling broth. Cook for a short time.
7. Pour equal part of soy sauce and lemon juice into 4 individual bowls. Lift cooked food out of the broth with a slotted spoon and place in the sauce bowl. Eat with the various condiments.

Note: To make *momiji-oroshi*, see pages 30, 95.

Japanese Menu with Tofu

1. *Iridofu* (Stir-Fried Tofu with Vegetables)
2. *Isobé-agé* (Deep-Fried Tofu with *Nori*)
3. *Agédashi-Dofu* (Deep-Fried Tofu)
4. *Shira-Aé* (White Salad)

1. *Iridofu* (Stir-Fried Tofu with Vegetables)

Ingredients:

1 cake tofu (½ lb., 225 g)
½ small carrot
2 *shiitake* (black mushrooms), dried
5 string beans
2 oz. (50 g) ground chicken

1 egg
2 tablespoons vegetable oil
2 tablespons soy sauce (*shoyu*)
1 tablespoon sugar
1 tablespoon *sake*

Method:

1. Wrap tofu in a cotton cloth and let stand for ½ hour.
2. Peel and cut the carrot into matchsticks. Soak *shiitake* in warm water for 20 minutes until soft. Drain, cut off stems and discard. Cut the caps in narrow strips. Parboil string beans and cut diagonally in narrow strips.
3. Heat oil in a wok or frying pan and sauté ground chicken, carrot and *shiitake* for 5 minutes. Season with soy sauce, sugar and *sake*.
4. Add tofu and stir-fry another 5 minutes, crumbling tofu with a spatula.
5. Beat the egg slightly and add to the tofu mixture, and stir-fry with 2 chopsticks until almost all the moisture has evaporated.
6. Add string beans and mix lightly.

2. *Isobé-Agé* (Deep-Fried Tofu with *Nori*)

Ingredients:

1 cake tofu (½ lb., 225 g)
Mixture A:
    4 oz. (120 g) cooked shrimp, minced
    1 spring onion, minced
    ½ egg, lightly beaten
    2 teaspoons sugar
    ¼ teaspoon salt
    1 tablespoon cornstarch
1 sheet *nori* (seaweed)

Oil for deep-frying
Mixture B:
    1 ½ tablespoons vinegar
    1 ½ tablespoons sugar
    1 tablespoon soy sauce (*shoyu*)
    3 tablespoons water
    1 teaspoon cornstarch, dissolved in 1 teaspoon water
    A few drops of fresh ginger juice

Method:

1. Boil tofu for 2 minutes. Then drain, wrap in a cotton cloth, and press to expel moisture. Grind in a *suribachi* (Japaneses mortar), or purée in a blender.
2. Combine ingredients of Mixture A. Mix them with the tofu. Heat oil for deep-frying.
3. Cut *nori* into 8 rectangles. Spread the tofu mixture on one side of the *nori*. Deep-fry in medium-hot oil 340°F. (170°C.), with the *nori*-side up. Turn once. Remove and keep warm.
4. Combine ingredients of mixture B in a saucepan. Bring to a boil, then add the dissolved cornstarch. When the sauce has thickened, stir in the ginger juice. Pour over the fried tofu, and serve immediately.

3. *Agédashi-Dofu* (Deep-Fried Tofu)

Ingredients:

3 cakes tofu (½ lb., 225 g each)
Cornstarch or flour
Oil for deep-frying
For dipping sauce:
    1 cup *dashi*
    ¼ cup *mirin*
    ¼ cup soy sauce (*shoyu*)

For garnishes:
    chopped chives or minced green onions
    bonito flakes
    grated *daikon* (giant white radish)
    grated fresh ginger
    lemon juice (optional)

Method:

1. Drain tofu on a bamboo mat (*sudaré*) for several hours. Cut each cake into 4 slices.
2. In a small saucepan, bring the ingredients for the dipping sauce to a boil.
3. Coat the pieces of tofu with cornstarch.
4. Heat the oil for deep-frying, but do not begin until the guests are seated. Deep-fry the tofu just until golden brown; do not overcook.

5. Pour the dipping sauce into small bowls—one for each guest. Put 3 pieces of tofu on a plate for each person. Sprinkle the bonito flakes and chives over the tofu. Place a small mound of grated *daikon* next to the tofu, and top the *daikon* with a bit of grated ginger. Serve immediately.

4. *Shira-Aé* (White Salad)

Ingredients:

½ cake tofu (¼ lb., 120 g)	1 tablespoon *mirin*
2 tablespoons white sesame seeds	3 red radishes
⅓ teaspoon salt	½ cucumber
1 tablespoon sugar	1 slice of cooked ham

Method:
1. Wrap tofu in a cotton cloth and place between two cutting boards. Raise one end of the boards several inches. Let sit for 30 minutes.
2. Toast the sesame seeds in a dry frying pan; shake the pan and remove as soon as they start to brown, for they burn easily. Place in a *suribachi* (Japanese mortar) and grind in a circular motion until the seeds are reduced to a fine paste. Add the tofu and grind the tofu and sesame paste together. Mix in the salt, sugar, and *mirin*. Press through a sieve or blend in a blender if a very smooth texture is desired.
3. Peel the cucumber, letting thin strips of the peel remain for decoration. Cut cucumber and radishes into paper-thin slices. Sprinkle with a little salt, and let stand until water is drawn out of them. Wrap in a towel and squeeze dry gently.
4. Cut ham into small squares.
5. Mix together the vegetables, ham, and tofu dressing. Serve chilled.

Notes:
1. In variations of this dish, a little vinegar is added to the tofu dressing. Also, vegetables such as carrots, string beans, and mushrooms, cut into matchsticks or thin slices and cooked, are often used.
2. It is important to dry all vegetables thoroughly before adding them to the dressing.

Chinese Menu with Tofu

1. Steamed Tofu Mold with Canadian Bacon
2. *Mabo-Dofu*
3. Deep-Fried Stuffed Vegetables
4. Tofu and Oyster Soup

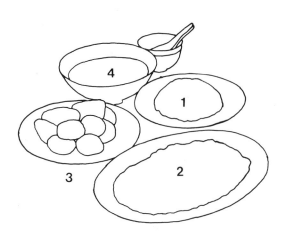

Chinese Menu with Tofu

1. Steamed Tofu Mold with Canadian Bacon

Ingredients:
12 oz. (360 g) tofu
7 oz. (200 g) Canadian bacon
6 large *shiitake*
1 thin slice of carrot, cut from the base of a large carrot
1 spring onion, chopped
1-inch (2.5 cm) piece of fresh ginger, peeled and sliced thinly
Vegetable oil
Sauce:
   2 tablespoons broth from steaming the tofu
   1 teaspoon each of soy sauce, *sake*, sesame oil, and cornstarch dissolved in 1 teaspoon water

Method:
1. Cut tofu crosswise into ¼-inch (6 mm) thick rectangles. Slice the Canadian bacon, and cut into strips, 1 ¼-inch (3 cm) wide. Wash *shiitake*, cut off stems, and cut into ½-inch (1 cm) strips. (If using dried *shiitake*, soak in warm water for 15 to 30 minutes until soft. Then proceed as above.) Cut the carrot slice into a flower, or use a decorative vegetable cutter now widely available.
2. For the mold use a small bowl with a diameter of about 8 inches (20 cm). Coat the inside with vegetable oil. Place the carrot flower in the center; then line the bowl with strips of tofu, *shiitake* and bacon alternately. Fill the bowl with the remaining tofu, *shiitake* and bacon. Sprinkle the top with the chopped spring onion and sliced ginger.
3. Place in a steamer, and steam over high heat for 20 minutes.
4. Gently pour 2 tablespoons of the broth out of the bowl. Combine in a small saucepan with all the other ingredients for the sauce. Bring to a boil, stirring constantly.
5. Unmold the contents by inverting the bowl onto a serving dish. Pour the sauce over it.

2. *Mabo-Dofu*

Ingredients:
2 cakes tofu (1 lb., 450 g)
1 cup lean ground pork or beef
1 teaspoon fresh ginger juice
1 teaspoon *sake*
1 teaspoon fresh ginger, minced
1 tablespoon white part of green onion, minced (reserve green part for garnish)
1 tablespoon garlic, minced
4 tablespoons lard or vegetable oil
Additional meat seasonings:
   1 teaspoon ground red pepper or cayenne

1 tablespoon *sake*
1 tablespoon *miso*
½ teaspoon salt
¼ cup soup stock
2 tablespoons cornstarch, dissolved in 2 tablespoons water

Method:
1. Boil tofu for 2–3 minutes. Let drain on a bamboo mat; then cut into ½-inch (1.5 cm) cubes.
2. Assemble and prepare the seasonings and other ingredients before beginning to cook. Combine the ginger juice and 1 teaspoon of *sake* with the ground meat.
3. Heat the lard in a wok or frying pan, and briefly stir-fry the minced ginger, garlic, and green onion. Add the meat, and stir-fry until the pork has become whitish or the beef has browned. Stir in the additional meat seasonings.
4. Add the soup stock and bring to a boil. Thicken with the dissolved cornstarch. Gently stir in the tofu. Place in a serving bowl, and sprinkle with the reserved green part of the onion, chopped. Serve hot.

Note:
Mabo-dofu comes from the Szechuan province of China and, like many Szechuan dishes is peppery hot. Feel free to adjust the pepper to your taste, reducing it or even eliminating it.

3. Deep-Fried Stuffed Vegetables

Ingredients:
1 cake tofu (½ lb., 225 g)
12 fresh *shiitake* or dried *shiitake* (soaked in water until soft)
1 carrot
1 green onion
4 small green peppers
Tofu-Vegetable Seasonings:
   1 egg, lightly beaten
   1 teaspoon flour
   1 teaspoon cornstarch
   1 teaspoon sesame oil
   ½ teaspoon salt
   pepper to taste
Flour for dusting vegetables
Oil for deep-frying

Method:
1. Dice tofu roughly and parboil. Drain on a bamboo mat.
2. Remove and discard the stems of the *shiitake*. Set aside for stuffing the 8 best-shaped *shiitake*; mince the remaining 4. Also, mince the carrot and green onion.
3. Cut the green peppers in half lengthwise and remove seeds. Dust the inside of the peppers and the 8 reserved *shiitake* with flour.
4. Combine the tofu with the minced vegetables. Add the tofu-vegetable seasonings, and mix thoroughly. Stuff the *shiitake* and green pepper shells with the mixture.
5. Heat the oil. Deep-fry the stuffed vegetables over medium heat.

4. Tofu and Oyster Soup

Ingredients:
1 cake tofu (½ lb., 250 g)
5 oz. (150 g) pork
1 tablespoon dried shrimp
3 *shiitake*
5 oz. (150 g) oysters
1 green onion
2 tablespoons vegetable oil
1 tablespoon *sake*
1 teaspoon salt
4 cups soup stock
2 tablespoons cornstarch, dissolved in 2 tablespoons water
1 teaspoon sesame oil
Pepper
1 sheet *nori*

Method:
1. Several steps need to be taken well in advance. The pork should be sliced extremely thinly, then cut into thin strips; this is easier to do if you partially freeze the pork beforehand. The dried shrimp should be soaked in warm water 30 to 60 minutes. If using dried *shiitake*, soak them in warm water for 15 to 30 minutes.
2. Cut the tofu into a ½-inch (1.5 cm) dice. Wash the oysters in water to which a little salt has been added. Remove and discard the stems from the *shiitake*. Mince the *shiitake* and green onion.
3. Heat the vegetable oil in a wok or deep frying pan. Add the *shiitake*, green onion, strips of pork, and shrimp. Stir-fry for 2 or 3 minutes; then season with *sake* and salt.
4. Add the soup stock, then the tofu and oysters. Bring to a boil, skimming off the foam as it forms. Thicken with dissolved cornstarch. Add sesame oil and a little pepper, and turn off heat.
5. Crisp *nori* over a flame, crush, and sprinkle over the soup. Serve immediately.

Champroh
(Okinawa-Style Fried Tofu) ▷

Champroh (Okinawa-Style Fried Tofu)

To press tofu for champroh, sprinkle the cakes with a little salt, wrap tightly in a cotton cloth, and place a 1-or 2-pound (1 kg) weight over the cakes. Let sit until the thickness of the tofu is reduced by ⅓.

1. Champroh with Soybean Sprouts
2. Champroh with *Daikon*
3. Champroh with Pickled Shallots

1. Champroh with Soybean Sprouts

Ingredients:
2 cakes pressed tofu (1 lb., 450 g before pressing)
7 oz. (200 g) soybean sprouts
3–5 oz. (90–150 g) chives or green onions
2 ½ tablespoons vegetable oil
2 tablespoons *sake*
1 ½ teaspoons salt
1 teaspoon soy sauce (*shoyu*)

Method:
1. Cut chives into 2-inch (5 cm) lengths.
2. Crush the pressed tofu roughly, and fry in vegetable oil. Add the soybean sprouts and chives, and fry briefly. Stir in the *sake*, salt, and soy sauce. Raise the heat for a moment, cooking just until everything is thoroughly heated.

2. Champroh with *Daikon*

Ingredients:
2 cakes pressed tofu (1 lb., 450 g before pressing)
12 oz. *daikon* (giant white radish)
1½ teaspoons salt
Additional salt for preparing *daikon*
Several green leaves from the *daikon*
2 tablespoons vegetable oil
2 eggs, lightly beaten
2 teaspoons soy sauce (*shoyu*)

Method:
1. Shred the daikon, place in a colander, and sprinkle with salt. Mix the salt in with your hand, then press and squeeze between your fingers to soften it and remove the moisture.
2. Mince the *daikon* leaves.
3. Crush the pressed tofu, and fry in the vegetable oil. Stir in the *daikon* and *daikon* leaves.
4. Check seasoning, and add soy sauce and salt as needed. (You may not need much, depending upon the amount of salt used in Step 1.)
5. Pour in the eggs, stir, and remove from the heat.

3. Champroh with Pickled Shallots

Ingredients:
1 tablespoon dried cloud-ear mushrooms
2½ tablespoons vegetable oil
5 oz. *rakkyo* or pickled shallots
2 tablespoons bonito flakes
2 cakes pressed tofu (1 lb., 450 g before pressing)
1 teaspoon salt
1 tablespoon soy sauce (*shoyu*)

Method:
1. Soak cloud-ear mushrooms in warm water for 30 minutes. Then rinse and shred.
2. Heat vegetable oil and fry *rakkyo* or shallots. Add the shredded cloud-ear mushrooms and the bonito flakes.
3. Crush the pressed tofu, add to the vegetables, and cook for several minutes. Season with salt and soy sauce.

Dengaku (Grilled Tofu with *Nerimiso*)

Nerimiso is a sweet, simmered *miso* sauce which can be prepared in advance. It is delicious on steamed vegetables as well as on tofu.

Ingredients:
3 tablespoons *dashi*
½ cup white *miso*
1 tablespoon sugar
1 tablespoon *mirin*
1 egg yolk, lightly beaten
3 cakes tofu (½ lb., 225 g each)
12 sprigs *kinomé*, or 4 teaspoons minced parsley
3 tablespoons sesame seeds

Method:
1. Prepare *nerimiso*: Bring the *dashi*, *miso*, sugar, and *mirin* to a boil. Lower the heat, and simmer for 20 minutes, stirring constantly with a wooden spoon. Let cool slightly, then blend in the lightly beaten egg yolk. Mix thoroughly until you have a smooth paste. Divide into two equal portions. Toast the sesame seeds in a dry pan, shaking the pan and removing it from the heat as soon as the seeds start to brown. Grind the seeds and add to one portion of the *nerimiso*.
2. Wrap tofu in a dry cloth and let stand for 20 minutes. Cut each cake of tofu into 4 rectangles. Spread the *nerimiso* on one side of the pieces of tofu; use the plain sauce on half of the pieces, and the sesame-flavored sauce on the other half of the pieces.
3. Grill both sides over charcoal until brown and crisp. You can also cook in an oven broiler: place tofu on a lightly oiled baking sheet, and broil on both sides. Decorate with the *kinomé*.

Note:
Dengaku is traditionally served with skewers. When grilling over charcoal, skewer the pieces of tofu with double-pronged skewers, if available, or with two plain bamboo skewers. Place two bars on the grill, and rest the skewers on them. If using an oven, broil the tofu unskewered; if you like, you can skewer the tofu after broiling.

Gammodoki (Deep-Fried Tofu Patties)

Ingredients:
2 cakes tofu (1 lb., 450 g)
4 *shiitake* (black mushrooms)
1 medium-sized carrot
8 ginkgo nuts
2 tablespoons cornstarch
Salt
Vegetable oil for deep-frying

Method:
1. Wrap tofu in a large cloth and let sit for 20 minutes to remove excess moisture. Purée in a blender.
2. If using dried *shiitake*, soak in warm water until soft. Cut off and discard *shiitake* stems, and cut into thin strips. Peel carrot and cut into matchsticks. If using fresh ginkgo nuts, crack the hard shell and remove the nuts; drop into boiling water and boil for a few minutes, then drain and rub off the thin brown skin.
3. Thoroughly mix together the tofu, *shiitake*, carrot sticks, and cornstarch. Season with salt to taste. Shape into 8 balls; push a ginkgo nut into the center of each ball and smooth the tofu around it.
4. Heat the oil and deep-fry the tofu patties over high heat. Serve immediately with mustard.

Inari-Zushi (Vinegared Rice in *Agé* Pouches)

Inari-zushi is a typical and popular picnic food in Japan. It plays somewhat the same role as sandwiches in America.

Ingredients (for 20 pouches):
3 cups short- or medium-grain rice, uncooked
10 *agé*
1 tablespoon sesame seeds
Rice seasonings:
    4 ½ tablespoons vinegar
    2 tablespoons sugar
    2 teaspoons salt
Agé seasonings:
    ½ cup soy sauce (*shoyu*)
    ⅓ cup *sake*
    7 tablespoons sugar
    1 tablespoon *mirin* (optional)
Vinegared ginger slices as a garnish, see page 94

Method:
1. If using Japanese rice, wash and drain thoroughly. Cook in 3 ¼ cups of water. Unlike Western-style rice, which is cooked until each grain is dry and separate, this Japanese-style rice should be moist and firm. Combine the rice seasonings, and sprinkle over the rice while it is still warm. Stir the rice lightly with a wooden spoon; at the same time, fan the rice rapidly with the other hand to cool it as rapidly as possible. (If you don't have a fan, use a magazine, newspaper, or flat pot lid.) Let cool.
2. Cut the *agé* in half to form 2-inch (5 cm) squares. Insert your thumb into the opening and gently pull apart the two layers. Scald (see general instructions, p. 14). Turn 10 of the pouches inside out so that the soft white side is outermost.
3. Place the *agé* in a large sauce pan or large, deep frying pan. (You need to use a cooking vessel with a large, flat base so that the *agé* seasonings can be absorbed by all the pouches.) Combine the *agé* seasonings and pour over the pouches. Add ½ cup water and cook over low heat for about 30 minutes, until almost all the liquid has evaporated. Let *agé* cool in the liquid.
4. Toast the sesame seeds in a dry frying pan, shaking the pan and removing it from the stove as soon as the seeds begin to brown. Chop them roughly on a cutting board, and mix with the vinegared rice.
5. Shape the rice into balls with moistened hands and stuff the pouches. Fold the open end over, and press the pouch lightly so that it is nicely shaped. Serve, garnished with vinegared ginger slices.

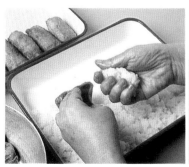  

Tsukimi-Dofu (Full-Moon Tofu)

Ingredients:

8 unshelled shrimp
4 *shiitake* (black mushrooms)
¼ lb. (120 g) boneless chicken breast
2 cakes tofu (½ lb., 225 g each)
4 egg yolks
3 cups *dashi*, seasoned with
   1½ tablespoons soy sauce (*shoyu*)

1½ tablespoons *mirin*
⅔ teaspoon salt
12 *mitsuba* sprigs, or cooked spinach
1 tablespoon cornstarch, dissolved in
   an equal amount of water
4 strips of lemon or *yuzu* peel

Method:

1. Devein and boil the shrimp in salted water. When cool enough to handle, remove shell, leaving the tail part attached. Cut off the tip of the tail. Cut off and discard the *shiitake* stems; cut into 2 or 3 pieces. (If using dried *shiitake*, pre-soak in warm water until softened.) Cut the chicken into small, very thin slices by holding the knife so that the blade is almost horizontal to the chicken. Draw the knife towards you, cutting off a 2-inch (5 cm) slice.
2. Bring water to a boil in a steamer. Cut the tofu cakes in half. Using a teaspoon, scoop out a hollow in the center; place an egg yolk in each hollow. Place in 4 individual soup bowls and steam over high heat for 3–4 minutes until tofu is heated through and egg yolk is soft boiled.
3. While the tofu is steaming, bring the seasoned *dashi* to a boil. Cook the *shiitake* and chicken for a few minutes, then remove with a slotted spoon.
4. Divide the shrimp, *shiitake*, chicken and *mitsuba* among the 4 soup bowls, arranging them around the tofu.
5. Thicken the remaining *dashi* with the dissolved cornstarch, and pour over the tofu. Garnish with strip of lemon peel. Cover the bowls, and let sit for several minutes before serving.

Stir-Fried Tofu, Shrimp and Peas

Ingredients:

½ lb. (225 g) shrimp
1 teaspoon ginger juice
2 teaspoons cornstarch
½ cup peas, fresh or frozen
1 cake tofu (½ lb., 230 g)

3 tablespoons lard
1 tablespoon *sake*
1 tablespoon soy sauce (*shoyu*)
Salt and pepper

Method:

1. Wash shrimp; remove shell and devein. Soak for 30 minutes in a solution of 2 cups water and 2 teaspoons salt to give them a crisp texture. Drain, sprinkle with the ginger juice and cornstarch, and stir well.
2. If using fresh peas, parboil. Defrost frozen peas.
3. Cut tofu into 8 pieces.
4. Melt 2 tablespoons of the lard in a heated wok or frying pan. Add the shrimp and the *sake*. Stir-fry until the shrimp have become pink. Remove with a slotted spoon.
5. Melt the remaining tablespoon of lard. Add the tofu, soy sauce and pepper to taste, and stir-fry. Add the peas and stir-fry for 1 or 2 more minutes. Return shrimp to the wok, and toss the ingredients just until the shrimp are heated through.

Tofu with Vegetables and Eggs

Ingredients:

2–3 eggs
Salt and pepper
2 tablespoons vegetable oil
3–4 *shiitake*
1 medium-sized carrot
8 oz. (240 g) string beans
1 green onion
2–3 cakes tofu (1–1½ lb., 450–675 g)

2–3 tablespoons vegetable oil
Vegetable seasonings:
  1 tablespoon *sake*
  ½ teaspoon sugar
  ⅓ teaspoon salt
  1 tablespoon soy sauce (*shoyu*)
  ½ teaspoon sesame oil

Method:

1. Beat eggs lightly and season with salt and pepper. Heat 2 tablespoons of the vegetable oil in a wok or frying pan and make soft scrambled eggs.
2. Soak dried *shiitake* in warm water until soft; cut off and discard the stems, and cut the caps into narrow strips. Peel the carrot and cut into matchsticks. Parboil string beans and cut diagonally into narrow strips. Mince the green onion.
3. Dice the tofu into ½-inch (1.5 cm) cubes. Slide them gently into boiling water, and bring the water back to a boil. Drain the tofu and let cool.
4. Heat a second wok or frying pan. Add 2–3 tablespoons vegetable oil. When hot, add the green onion and stir-fry thoroughly. Add *shiitake* and carrots, and stir-fry for another minute or two. Add the vegetable seasonings, and stir all the ingredients together. After several broad stirring motions, add the tofu and string beans. Continue to stir-fry until all the liquid is absorbed. Add the scrambled eggs, breaking up the clumps. Mix everything together thoroughly and quickly; do not overcook.

Eight-Treasure Tofu

Ingredients:

2 cakes tofu (½ lb., 225 g each)
¼ lb. (120 g) shrimp
¼ lb. (120 g) pork, thinly sliced
4 large *shiitake*
2 green onions
¼ lb. (120 g) bamboo shoots
20 snow peas
4 tablespoons vegetable oil
½ cup soup stock
1 egg, lightly beaten
Seasonings:
  For the shrimp:
    ½ teaspoon ginger juice
    ½ tablespoon cornstarch
    ½ teaspoon salt

For the pork:
  ½ teaspoon ginger juice
  ½ teaspoon *sake*
  pinch of salt
Stir-frying Seasonings:
  1 tablespoon *sake*
  1 ⅓ teaspoons salt
  ½ teaspoon sugar
  1 teaspoon soy sauce (*shoyu*)
Finishing touch:
  1 tablespoon cornstarch, dissolved in
    an equal amount of water
  1 teaspoon sesame oil

Method:

1. Grate fresh ginger and squeeze it to obtain 1 teaspoon juice which will be divided between the shrimp and pork. Dissolve the cornstarch. Set out the other seasonings.
2. Cut tofu into ¾-inch (2 cm) cubes. Place in boiling water; let the water come back to a boil, then drain and place in cold water to prevent the cubes from sticking together.
3. Shell and devein shrimp, and wash in salt water. Mix thoroughly with the shrimp seasonings.
4. Cut the pork slices into 1-inch (2.5 cm) squares, and mix thoroughly with the pork seasonings.
5. Cut off and discard *shiitake* stems; cut in quarters. (If using dried *shiitake*, pre-soak in warm water until soft.) Cut green onions into 1-inch (2.5 cm) lengths, and the bamboo shoots into 1-inch (2.5 cm) squares. String the snow peas and parboil in salted water.
6. Heat a wok or frying pan. Add the vegetable oil. When the oil is hot, add the *shiitake* and green onions, and stir-fry until well coated with oil. Next, add the pork and stir-fry for 1 or 2 minutes. Finally, add the shrimp and bamboo shoots, and again stir-fry for a minute or two.
7. Add the stir-frying seasonings, and give the ingredients a few turns so that the seasonings are evenly distributed. Pour in the soup stock.
8. Drain the tofu and pat dry with a towel. Add to the vegetable mixture. Check the seasonings, adding more salt if needed. Bring to a boil.
9. Pour in the egg in a sweeping motion and quickly stir it into the ingredients.
10. For the finishing touch, add dissolved cornstarch to the pan, cooking until the sauce has thickened. Sprinkle with sesame oil, then scatter the snow peas over the surface, and serve hot.

Five-Colored Fried Tofu

Ingredients:
1 lb. (450 g) tofu
1 small stalk of celery
2 oz. (60 g) carrot
2 oz. (60 g) green pepper
3 *shiitake*, fresh or dried
1 egg, beaten
½ teaspoon sugar
1 teaspoon salt
2 teaspoons sesame oil
4 tablespoons flour
Vegetable oil for deep-frying
Ketchup and Szechuan pepper-salt (see glossary)

Method:
1. Press tofu with a light weight.
2. Mince vegetables and *shiitake*. When dried *shiitake* are used, prepare them according to the instruction given in the glossary.
3. In a large bowl combine all the ingredients except the last two. Knead thoroughly. Add a little more flour if the mixture is too soft.
4. In a frying pan or wok heat the oil to 350°F. (180°C.). Drop spoonfuls of the mixture into it and fry to a golden color.
5. Serve hot with ketchup and Szechuan pepper-salt.

Tofu-*Chawanmushi*

Chawanmushi is a non-sweet custard which can be served instead of a soup. It is equally good hot or cold. Special *chawanmushi* cups with lids are often available in many gourmet kichen shops and oriental markets. You may also use any heatproof cup or mug. Western custard cups are generally not tall enough to show this dish off to the best advantage; however, use them in a pinch, for *chawanmushi* is too good to pass up.

Ingredients:
1 cake tofu (½ lb., 225 g)
2 eggs, lightly beaten
20 ginkgo nuts
4 shrimp
4 *shiitake*
12 stalks *mitsuba* (or young spinach leaves)
Seasonings:
    1½ cup *dashi* (or chicken stock)
    1 tablespoon light soy sauce (*usukuchi shoyu*)
    1 teaspoon *mirin*
    ⅓ teaspoon salt

Method:
1. Rinse off tofu and wrap in a cotton cloth. Press between two cutting boards. Purée the tofu in a blender.
2. Thoroughly mix together the tofu, eggs, and seasonings.
3. If using fresh ginkgo nuts, crack and remove the hard, white shells. Drop into lightly salted boiling water, then remove the thin brown skins. Cook the shrimp in lightly salted boiling water. If using dried *shiitake*, soak in warm water until soft; cut off and discard stems. Cut *mitsuba* into 1-inch (2.5 cm) lengths.
4. Pour water into steamer and set over high heat.
5. Divide tofu-egg mixture among 4 cups. Place 5 ginkgo nuts in each cup and arrange a mushroom and shrimp on top.
6. Place the cups in the steamer; do not cover them. Wrap the lid of the steamer in a dish towel which will absorb the moisture that collects, preventing it from dripping onto the custard. Be sure to secure the ends of the towel firmly on top of the lid to keep them away from the fire. Cook over high heat for 2 minutes. Then reduce heat and tilt the lid so that the steamer is slightly uncovered. Steam gently for 12–15 minutes. Shortly before the custard is set, decorate the tops with the *mitsuba*.
7. To check, insert a toothpick, into the center; the soup will come out clear when it is done. If using *chawanmushi* cups, cover before serving. This is one of the few Japanese dishes eaten with both a spoon and chopsticks.

Variation:
Try garnishing with crumbled *nori* and grated *wasabi* (Japanese green horseradish).

Gisei-Dofu (Buddhist Monks' Frittata)

Gisei-dofu is named after a nun called *Gisei* who invented the dish. The following recipe includes eggs which the original version did not call for.

Ingredients:
2 cakes tofu (1 lb., 450 g)
2 *shiitake*
2 oz. (60 g) carrots
2 tablespoons peas, fresh or frozen
2 eggs, lightly beaten
Vegetable oil
Vegetable seasonings:
    ¼ cup water from soaking the *shiitake*
    2 teaspoons sugar
    1 tablespoon soy sauce (*shoyu*)
Tofu-egg seasonings:
    ½ teaspoon salt
    1 teaspoon *mirin*
    2 teaspoons sugar

Method:
1. Break the tofu into small pieces. Place in boiling water and cook for 1 or 2 minutes. Pour into a colander lined with a large cloth. Draw up the corners of the cloth to form a sack, and press to expel liquid. Use the bottom of a glass to press the tofu if it is too hot to touch.
2. Wash the *shiitake* and peel the carrot. Dice both into ⅛ inches (5 mm) cubes. Place in a small saucepan with the vegetable seasonings, and cook until all the liquid has evaporated.
3. Cook the peas in salt water. Drain.
4. Grind the tofu in a *suribachi* (Japanese mortar) or purée in a blender. Gradually add the lightly beaten eggs and mix thoroughly. Stir in the tofu-egg seasonings. Add the *shiitake*, carrots, and peas. Mix well.
5. Heat a rectangular or square pan and coat it with vegetable oil. Place the tofu mixture in the pan. Turn the heat very low and cook, covered, until the mixture is almost set. Turn with a broad spatula and cook until completely firm. Cool in the pan.
6. When the *gisei-dofu* is completely cool, cut into ½ inch (1.5 cm) slices. Garnish serving dish with pickled ginger shoots, if desired.

Note:
Although this dish is traditionally made in a square or rectangular pan, a round pie tin could also be used; cut into wedges instead of slices. *Gisei-dofu* may also be baked in a preheated 350°F. (180°C.) oven for about 30 minutes.

Agé-Rolls with Meat Stuffing

Ingredients:

2 *agé* (2 × 4 inches, 5 × 10 cm each)
3–4 *kikurage* (cloud-ear mushrooms) or
   shiitake (black mushrooms)
½ lb. (225 g) lean ground pork
½ cup bread crumbs, moistened with a little water
1 egg
1 tablespoon cornstarch

Meat binder and seasonings:
   1 tablespoon cornstarch
   1 teaspoon grated fresh ginger
   2 teaspoons soy sauce (*shoyu*)
   ⅛ teaspoon pepper
Serving condiment: mustard

Method:

1. Pour hot water over *agé* to remove excess oil. Cut a thin strip off both short ends and one of the long ends. Insert thumb and gently open *agé* out into a single layer. Mince the cut-off strips of *agé* and set aside until Step 3.
2. If using dried *shiitake*, soak in warm water until soft. Cut off and discard stems; cut into thin strips.
3. Mix the pork with the minced *agé*, *kikurage* or *shiitake*, and moistened bread crumbs. Add the meat binder and seasonings, and mix well.
4. Separate the egg. Measure off half of the egg white and set aside until Step 6. Add the other half of the white and the yolk to the meat mixture. Knead it firmly until it becomes smooth.
5. Bring water to a boil in a steamer. Roll the meat into two sausages the same length as that of the *agé* sheets. Wrap the sausages tightly in damp cloths, and steam over high heat in a preheated steamer for about 25 minutes. Let cool.
6. Combine the reserved ½ egg white with 1 tablespoon water and 1 tablespoon cornstarch.
7. Spread the *agé* on a cutting board with the white, unfried surface facing upward. Brush with the egg white-cornstarch mixture. Place a meat roll on each *agé*, and roll up tightly. To seal the *agé* roll, moisten the edge with the egg white-cornstarch mixture and press down; fasten with toothpicks.
8. Heat oil for deep-frying. Deep-fry the *agé*-rolls over very high heat. Cut into ⅓-inch (1 cm) slices, and serve hot with mustard.

Pork in *Agé* Pouches

Ingredients: (for 8 pouches)

4 *agé*
6 cups shredded *daikon* (white radish)
Salt
16 stalks *mitsuba*
½ lb. (230 g) lean ground pork

1 tablespoon fresh ginger, minced
2 cups *dashi*
3 tablespoons soy sauce (*shoyu*)
1 tablespoon sugar
12 ginkgo nuts, canned

Method:

1. Cut *agé* in half, forming 2-inch (5 cm) squares. Gently pull the cut edges apart to form a pouch. Scald (see general instructions, p. 14).
2. Sprinkle salt over shredded *daikon*. Let sit until the water is drawn out. Rinse and press firmly to remove moisture.
3. If using *mitsuba*, parboil until the stems become pliable.

4. Mix together shredded *daikon*, pork, and minced ginger; fill the *agé* pouches with the mixture. Tie the open end of the pouch with a *mitsuba* stalk (or with kitchen twine if *mitsuba* is unavailable). Reserve the extra *mitsuba* for garnish.
5. Bring the *dashi* to a boil, and add the soy sauce and sugar. Place the *agé* pouches and ginkgo nuts in the saucepan, and simmer over low heat for 30 minutes. Before serving, garnish with the reserved *mitsuba*, cut into 1-inch (2.5 cm) pieces. If you have tied the pouches with string, remove string before serving; garnish with celery leaves.

Vinegared *Okara* with Marinated Fish

Ingredients:

½ mackerel, fileted
Up to 4 tablespoons salt
1 cup + 4 tablespoons vinegar
1 cup water
1-inch (2.5 cm) piece of fresh ginger
1 cup *okara*

Okara seasonings:
  2 tablespoons salt
  1 tablespoon vinegar
1 egg yolk
1 small cucumber

Method:

1. Carefully go over the mackerel, removing all the small bones; an eyebrow tweezer is useful for this. Cover the filet with a generous amount of salt; let sit for 5 hours.
2. Peel the ginger and cut into very thin slices. Cut half of the slices lengthwise into threads; reserve for the final garnish.
3. Wash the salt from the mackerel with a solution of vinegar and water (1 cup vinegar to 1 cup water). Turn the mackerel skin-side up, pour the remaining of 4 tablespoons vinegar over it, and sprinkle with the sliced ginger. Let sit for 1 hour. Then skin and cut into thin slices, about 5 to the inch.
4. Heat the *okara* seasonings; add the *okara* and cook until fluffy, stirring constantly. Add the egg yolk, and continue to cook and stir for several more minutes. Let cool completely.
5. Cut the cucumber in half lengthwise; then slice thinly. Mix with a little salt; press and squeeze to expel the water. Rinse with vinegar, and squeeze dry.
6. Mix together the mackerel, *okara*, and cucumber. To serve, divide among 4 bowls, and garnish with ginger threads.

Sautéed *Okara* with Vegetables

Ingredients:

2 *shiitake* (black mushrooms)
1 small carrot
4 inches (10 cm) of green onion (green part only)
10 string beans
Salt
2 cups *dashi*
3 tablespoons soy sauce (*shoyu*)

3 tablespoons sugar
2 tablespoons sesame oil
2 cups *okara*
1 egg
2 teaspoons *mirin*
Shredded *nori*

Method:

1. If using fresh *shiitake*, wash them, cut off stems, and cut into thin strips. If using dried *shiitake*, soak them in warm water for about 15 minutes until soft; then proceed as with fresh *shiitake*.
2. Cut carrot into matchsticks. Slice the string beans and green onion lengthwise into thin strips.
3. Cook the *shiitake*, carrots, and green onions in the *dashi* seasoned with the soy sauce and sugar. After 10 minutes remove from stove and let cool in the *dashi*.
4. Cook the string beans in salted water for 5 minutes; then drain.
5. Heat the sesame oil in a skillet, add the *okara* and cook until it becomes dry and fluffy. Add the vegetables and *dashi* from Step 3 and cook over low heat, stirring constantly to prevent burning, until most of the liquid has evaporated.

6. Beat the egg lightly and stir rapidly into the *okara* mixture. Add string beans, *mirin* and cook another 5 minutes.
7. Mound the *okara* in a bowl, and let cool to room temperature. Garnish with *nori* just before serving.

Koya-Dofu with *Shiitake* and Snow Peas

Ingredients:
4 cakes *koya-dofu*
4 dried *shiitake*
4 oz. (120 g) snow peas
For simmering *koya-dofu*:
   2 cups *dashi*
   4 tablespoons sugar
   1 teaspoon salt
   1 tablespoon soy sauce (*shoyu*)
For simmering *shiitake*:
   ¼ cup water in which *shiitake* were soaked
   ¼ cup broth in which *koya-dofu* was simmered
   1 tablespoon soy sauce (*shoyu*)
   1 tablespoon sugar
Salt
Mirin
A sprig of *kinomé* or other small green leaves

Method:
1. Soak *koya-dofu* in warm water for 20 minutes; turn the cakes over several times. When *koya-dofu* has doubled in size, cut one cake in half; if there is still a hard, white line in the middle, soak a little longer. When completely soft, drain and place in cold water to cover. Press between the palms, expelling a cloudy liquid. Change the water and press again; repeat until the water remains clear.
2. Cut each cake of *koya-dofu* into 4 slices, and place in a single layer in a saucepan with the ingredients for simmering *koya-dofu*. Place a drop-lid on the *koya-dofu* to ensure even penetration of the flavorings: in Japan a wooden drop-lid (*otoshi-buta*) is used, but any heatproof plate or flat pot-lid just small enough to fit inside the saucepan will do. Bring to a boil, then reduce heat to low and simmer until ⅓ of the liquid has evaporated. Cool in the broth.
3. Soak *shiitake* in warm water until soft; then cut off and discard stems. Place in the seasoned liquid for simmering *shiitake*, and cook over low heat for 15 minutes. Cool in the liquid.
4. String the snow peas. Cook in boiling salted water for 5 minutes. Drain, then sprinkle with salt and a dash of *mirin*.
5. Arrange all the ingredients on a serving dish, and serve at room temperature.

Monk's *Tempura*

A delicious vegetarian dish with yuba and two kinds of seaweed, as well as traditional vegetables.

Ingredients:

4 *shiitake* or white mushrooms
1 sweet potato
1 small lotus root
1 carrot
2 green peppers
4 fresh ginger shoots (*ha-shoga*), if available
1 sheet of *nori* (optional)
8 inches (20 cm) *kombu*
4 *yuba* rolls and 20 pieces of thin noodles
1 teaspoon black sesame seeds for dusting sweet potato (optional)

Batter:
1 cup sifted cake flour
1 egg
1 cup cold water
1 tablespoon *sake*
pinch of salt
Dipping sauce:
1 cup *dashi*
¼ cup *mirin*
¼ cup soy sauce (*shoyu*)
½ cup grated *daikon* (white radish)
Oil for deep-frying

Method:

1. Clean the *shiitake* or mushrooms. Discard the stems. If very large, cut in half.
2. Peel the sweet potato, lotus root, and carrot. Cut into ¼-inch (6 mm) slices. Place the lotus root in vinegar-water to prevent discoloration. Slant the knife when cutting the carrot so that the slices are about 2 inches (5 cm) long.
3. Cut the green peppers into quarters and remove seeds.
4. Cut the *nori* into 2-inch (5 cm) squares. Cut *kombu* into strips ½-inch (1 cm) wide and 2-inch (5 cm) long. Tie each of the strips in a decorative knot by making a loop, passing one end through the loop and pulling it tight.
5. Heat about 5 cups of vegetable oil to 350°F. (180°C.).
6. While the oil is heating, deep-fry the *yuba* and *kombu*. These ingredients need to be fried slowly, at a low temperature. They should not be coated with the *tempura* batter.
7. Also, while the oil is heating, prepare the *tempura* batter. Beat the egg lightly; add water, *sake*, and salt. Sift in the flour; stir briskly and briefly: the batter should remain lumpy.
8. Dry the vegetables thoroughly, then dip into the batter. Sprinkle the sweet potato slices with black sesame seeds. Over medium-low heat, deep-fry the vegetables immediately after coating each slice. Do not crowd the vegetables in the oil: no more than 80% of the surface of the oil should be covered in order to maintain a constant temperature.
9. Drain the vegetables on a grid. (Two cake coolers stacked at right angles will do nicely.)
10. Dipping sauce: Bring *dashi*, *mirin* and soy sauce to a boil.
11. *Tempura* is traditionally served on a bamboo plate covered with a piece of the Japanese paper called *washi*. You can substitute an ordinary chinaware plate for the bamboo; use a plain white paper napkin for the *washi*. Pour the dipping sauce into small bowls, one for each diner, and place a mound of grated *daikon* in each. The guests mix the *daikon* into the sauce, and dip the *tempura* into the mixture.

Note:

Other vegetables can also be used for *tempura*: for example, eggplant, string beans, ginkgo nuts, and celery.

Tofu Steak

Ingredients
4 cakes tofu (½ lb., 225 g each)
2 large cloves garlic, grated
½ cup soy sauce (*shoyu*)
Topping:
    ½ cup finely chopped *zha-cai* (Szechuan preserved vegetable)
    4 tablespoons black sesame seeds, toasted in a dry pan, then minced
⅓ cup vegetable oil

Method:
1. Wrap each piece of tofu in a dry cloth; drain for 4–5 hours on a slanted cutting board.
2. Mix the garlic and soy sauce.
3. Heat the oil. Slip in the tofu and cook over high heat for several minutes; then reduce the heat. With chopsticks, stab many holes in the cakes of tofu; slowly pour ⅔ of the garlic-soy sauce mixture over tofu, letting it sink into the holes. When the bottom of the tofu is nicely brown, turn, pour on the remainder of the garlic-soy sauce, and cook for a few more minutes.
4. Place on a plate with the side that was browned first on top. Spread the topping over the tofu cakes.

Cabbage Rolls with Tofu Filling

Ingredients:

2 cakes tofu (½ lb., 225 g each)
2 *shiitake* (black mushrooms)
2 green onions
Meat seasonings:
   1 tablespoon *sake*
   2 tablespoons soy sauce (*shoyu*)
   1 ½ tablespoons sugar
   1 teaspoon fresh ginger, minced

8 oz. (240 g) ground beef
2 tablespoons cornstarch
8 large cabbage leaves
1 tablespoon cornstarch for dusting cabbage leaves
2 cups *dashi*
Dashi seasonings:
   2 tablespoons soy sauce (*shoyu*)
   2 tablespoons sugar

Method:

1. Crumble tofu by placing in a dry cloth, drawing up the ends to form a sack, and squeezing. If using dried *shiitake*, soak in warm water until soft; then cut off and discard stems. Mince the *shiitake* and green onion.
2. Bring the meat seasonings to a boil, and add the ground beef, *shiitake* and green onion. Cook for several minutes. Take off the stove and let cool, then stir in the tofu and 2 tablespoons cornstarch.
3. Cut away the hard core of the cabbage leaves; parboil, drain, and pat dry with a towel.
4. To assemble, sprinkle the inside of the leaves with cornstarch; place ⅛ of the tofu-meat filling at the thick end of each leaf and fold like an envelope. Fasten with a toothpick.
5. Bring to a boil the *dashi* and *dashi* seasonings. Put the cabbage rolls in the pan in a single layer. Place a drop-lid over the rolls (page 16). Simmer for ½ hour.
6. Place cabbage rolls in a serving dish and keep warm. Thicken the remaining sauce with the dissolved cornstarch, and pour it over the cabbage rolls. Serve hot.

Deep-Fried Tofu with Cheese Stuffing

Ingredients:

2 cakes tofu (½ lb., 225 g each)
4 slices cheese (any type that melts well)
Fine dry bread crumbs for coating
3 tablespoons grated Parmesan cheese
Flour for coating
1 egg, lightly beaten
Oil for deep-frying

Garnishes:
   tomato wedges
   shredded cabbage
   parsley
Condiments:
   ketchup
   Worcestershire sauce

Method:

1. Wrap each cake of tofu in a dry cloth; cover with a light weight and let sit for an hour.
2. Cut the tofu cakes in half. Slide a sharp knife into the tofu parallel to the largest surface; make a slit, leaving a border of ½ inch (1 cm) on 3 sides. Insert a slice of cheese into each slit.
3. Mix bread crumbs and Parmesan cheese. Heat the oil for deep-frying.
4. Coat the tofu with flour, dip in the egg, then coat with bread crumbs. Deep-fry quickly in hot oil.
5. Place on a plate with the garnishes, and serve with ketchup and Worcestershire sauce.

Italian-Style Tofu with Tomatoes

Ingredients:
3 cakes tofu (½ lb., 225 g each)
Salt and pepper
3 ripe tomatoes, or 1 lb. (450 g) canned, peeled tomatoes
1 clove garlic
3 shallots
1 onion
3 tablespoons olive oil
3 tablespoons butter
1 tablespoon tomato paste
½ cup dry white wine
½ cup water
2 bouillon cubes
1 bay leaf
Flour for dusting
Minced parsley for garnishing

Method:
1. Sprinkle salt and pepper over tofu and let stand until the water comes out. Drain in a colander.
2. Peel tomatoes, cut in half, and squeeze firmly to remove seeds. Dice.
3. Peel garlic and shallots; mince, keeping them in separate piles. Cut onion into thin slices.
4. In a heavy saucepan, heat 1 ½ tablespoons each of the olive oil and butter. Fry the onion and shallots until golden. Stir in the garlic and tomato paste and cook for several more minutes.
5. Add the wine and bring to a boil. Then add ½ cup water, the bouillon cubes, bay leaf, and tomatoes.
6. Cut the tofu into ½-inch (1.5 cm) slices; dust with flour.
7. In a second pan, heat the remaining 1 ½ tablespoons olive oil and butter. Sauté the tofu until golden brown.
8. Slide the tofu into the tomato-sauce, and simmer over low heat until the sauce thickens. Serve sprinkled with minced parsley.

Tofu-Burgers

Ingredients:

2 cakes tofu (½ lb., 225 g each)
2 medium-sized potatoes
¼ cup shredded carrot (optional)
¼ cup shredded *shiitake* (optional)
¼ cup minced onion
1 tablespoon minced parsley

Salt and pepper
Nutmeg
Sugar
4 tablespoons vegetable oil
1 tablespoon minced chives or spring onions
1 teaspoon toasted, minced sesame seeds

Method:

1. Press tofu between 2 cutting boards. Raise one end a few inches so that the water will drain. Pat tofu dry with a towel. Using a fork, break into small pieces, then mash until smooth. Season with salt, pepper, nutmeg, and a pinch of sugar.
2. Peel potatoes and grate, using the finest side of a grater. Place in a towel, and draw up the corners to form a sack; twist and press until dry.
3. Thoroughly mix together the tofu, potatoes, shredded carrots and *shiitake*, onion, and parsley. Season again with salt and pepper, if necessary. Shape into 4 patties.
4. Heat the vegetable oil; fry the tofu patties over medium heat in a covered pan. Turn to brown the other side, covering pan again.
5. Sprinkle with the chives and sesame seeds, and serve hot with mustard.

Baked Eggplant with Tofu Filling

Ingredients:

1 cake tofu (½ lb., 225 g)
4 small eggplants, 5–6 inches (12–15 cm) long
¼ lb. (112 g) cream cheese
2 teaspoons cornstarch
Salt and pepper
Nutmeg
Vegetable oil

Method:

1. Wrap tofu in a dry cloth: drain for ½ hour on a cutting board.
2. Cut eggplants in half lengthwise. Scoop out the flesh with a spoon, leaving a ½-inch (1 cm) shell. Preheat the oven to 350°F. (180°C.).
3. Finely chop the scooped-out flesh, and sprinkle with 1 teaspoon salt. Mix well with your hands, and squeeze out the water.
4. Crumble the tofu and mix with the chopped eggplant. Blend in the cream cheese with your fingers. Add the cornstarch and mix thoroughly. Season with salt, pepper, and nutmeg.
5. Stuff the eggplant shells with the filling. Brush the tops with vegetable oil. Bake in the pre-heated oven for 25 minutes.

Note:

Small eggplants are sometimes available in supermarkets, especially during the summer. You can generally find them in Oriental, Italian, and Middle-eastern food stores.

77
77

Chef Salad with Tofu

Ingredients:
1 cake tofu (½ lb., 225 g)
½ clove garlic
1 small head lettuce
½ cup diced cucumber
½ cup diced celery
½ cup diced green pepper
½ cup diced Swiss cheese
1 cup diced cooked meat (such as chicken, beef, ham, pork)
½ cup diced cooked carrot
For dressing:
  ⅔ cup salad oil
  ⅓ cup vinegar or 3 teaspoons lemon juice
  3 tablespoons minced onion
  Salt, pepper and sugar

Method:
1. Place tofu in boiling water. When the tofu begins to sway, drain and wrap in a dry towel. Let sit for ½ hour.
2. Cut tofu into ½-inch (1 cm) cubes.
3. Rub chilled salad bowl with garlic. Tear lettuce into bite-sized pieces, and combine in the salad bowl with all the other ingredients.
4. To make the dressing, mix the minced onion with oil and vinegar. Season with salt, pepper, and a pinch of sugar. Just before serving, mix thoroughly and pour over the salad. Toss the salad gently so as not to crush the tofu.

Green Herb Sauce

Ingredients:
1 cake tofu (½ lb., 225 g)
½ cup yogurt
¼ cup mayonnaise
3 tablespoons minced onion
3 hard boiled eggs, minced
1 cup minced herbs such as parsley, spinach, watercress, chervil, chives, etc.
¼ cup sour cucumber pickles, minced
1 tablespoon mustard
¼ cup lemon juice
Salt, pepper and sugar
Boiled or baked potatoes

Method:
1. Beat tofu with a hand mixer until smooth.
2. Blend in all the other ingredients and mix thoroughly. Season with salt, pepper and a pinch of sugar. Just before serving pour green sauce over hot potatoes.

Salad with Tofu Dressing

Ingredients:
¼ cake tofu (⅛ lb., 60 g)
¼ cup mayonnaise
¼ cup yogurt
1 teaspoon mustard
1 tablespoon lemon juice
salt and pepper
1 small cucumber
2 small green peppers
4-inch (10 cm) stalk celery
1 small carrot

Method:
1. Put tofu into boiling water. When it begins to sway, drain and pat dry with a towel. Beat in a mixer until smooth.
2. Combine mayonnaise, yogurt, mustard, lemon juice and tofu. Stir until smooth, and season with salt and pepper.
3. Cut the vegetables into matchsticks. Mix well, and place in a chilled bowl. Pour over the tofu-dressing just before serving.

Jellied Dessert in Two Colors

Ingredients:
1 stick of agar (¼ oz., 8 g)
½ lb. (225 g) tofu
3 tablespoons sugar
2 drops of almond extract
2 tablespoons creme de menthe

Method:
1. Wash agar and soak in 2 cups of water for ½ hour or longer.
2. Parboil tofu and press with a heavy weight for ½ hour. Crumble and beat in a blender with the sugar until smooth.
3. For the molds, use 2 rectangular pans of about 3 × 5 inches (7.5 × 12.5 cm), or any ½ quart (0.5 *l*) dish. Rinse the molds with cold water, and divide the puréed tofu between the two. Sprinkle the creme de menthe over 1 portion and the almond extract over the other. Blend well.
4. Remove the agar from the water, and press it firmly to squeeze out the liquid. In a saucepan combine agar with a little water and bring to a boil. Simmer for a few minutes, stirring constantly, until agar dissolves. Press through a strainer onto the tofu, dividing it equally between the two molds. Mix well. Chill in the refrigerator.
5. When the jelly has become firm, unmold and cut each cake into quarters. To serve, place 1 piece of the almond jelly and 1 piece of the creme de menthe jelly on each dish.

Caramelized Custard

Ingredients:
8 tablespoons sugar
8 tablespoons water
10 oz. (330 g) tofu, coarsely crumbled
3 eggs
½ cup sugar
1 teaspoon vanilla extract
2 cups milk
1 tablespoon cornstarch
Vegetable oil

Method:
1. Preheat oven to 375°F. (190°C.). Prepare a baking dish which holds 1¼ quarts (1.2*l*) by coating it with vegetable oil.
2. Combine the sugar and water in a small saucepan. Bring to a boil, then reduce heat to low and cook until the syrup becomes golden brown. Quickly pour it into the baking dish, tilting the dish so that the whole bottom surface is coated. Set aside.
3. Combine all the other ingredients in a blender or mixer, and blend until smooth. Pour into the baking dish.
4. Pour hot water into a pan until it is half full, and set the custard dish into it. Bake for 40 minutes at 375°F. (190°C.).
5. Let cool, then unmold onto a serving dish.

Tofu-Pie

Ingredients:
Filling:
  2 cakes tofu (1 lb., 450 g), well drained
  3 tablespoons honey
  ¼ cup raisins, chopped
  ¼ cup lemon juice
  ½ teaspoon lemon extract
  ½ teaspoon vanilla extract
  Pinch of salt
  1 egg, well beaten
Crust:
  ¼ cup zwieback (rusk) crumbs
  ½ cup rolled oats
  2 teaspoons lemon juice
  2 teaspoons honey
  2 teaspoons butter
1 teaspoon butter to grease the pie tin

Method:
1. Preheat oven to 350°F. (180°C.). Beat tofu in a mixer until smooth. Place in a large bowl, add all the ingredients for the filling, and blend thoroughly.
2. Grease an 8-inch (20 cm) pie tin with butter.
3. Thoroughly blend the pie crust ingredients with the fingers. Press evenly against the bottom and sides of the pie tin.
4. Spoon filling over the crust; flatten the top.
5. Bake in a moderate oven for about 25 minutes. Cool completely before cutting.

Liver Loaf I

Ingredients

½ lb. (225 g) chicken livers
½ lb. (225 g) ground pork, beef, or chicken
¼ cup brandy
10 oz. (300 g) tofu
½ cup heavy cream
¼ cup bread crumbs
⅓ cup minced onion
1 tablespoon sweet marjoram

1 egg
⅓ cup dry instant cream of mushroom soup
½ teaspoon salt
A pinch of pepper
3–4 bay leaves
Vegetable oil
Butter

Method:

1. Preheat oven to 400°F. (204°C.).
2. Cut away the fat and veins of the livers. Wash in cold water, then pat dry with a kitchen towel.
3. Heat a frying pan and coat with a little vegetable oil. Fry the livers and ground meat until half done. Stir in the brandy, and season with salt and pepper. Cover and cook over low heat for 5–7 minutes.
4. Scrape the contents of the frying pan into a blender, and add all the other ingredients through the cream of mushroom soup mix. Blend to a smooth paste. Add more salt and pepper, if necessary.
5. Butter a 1¼ quart (1.2 *l*) loaf pan. Fill with the meat mixture, smoothing each spoonful with a spatula to avoid bubbles.
6. Smooth the top and decorate with the bay leaves.
7. Bake uncovered for 40 minutes.
8. To serve as an appetizer, cut into slices and serve warm on pieces of whole wheat or rye toast. It can also be used cold as a sandwich filler.

Liver Loaf II

This recipe uses more tofu than Liver Loaf I.

Ingredients:

½ lb. (225 g) chicken livers
¾ lb. (340 g) ground chicken,
    or half chicken and half pork
¼ cup brandy
1 ⅓ lb. (600 g) tofu
½ cup heavy cream
½ cup bread crumbs
⅓ cup minced onion
⅓ cup minced parsley

1 tablespoon dried marjoram
1 egg
½ cup dry instant cream of mushroom soup
1 teaspoon salt
A pinch of pepper
5 bay leaves
Vegetable oil
Butter

Method:

Follow the same directions as in the recipe for Liver Loaf I.

Tofu-Pineapple Bavarian

Ingredients:

1½ tablespoons unflavored gelatin
10 oz. (300 g) tofu
⅓ cup sugar
⅔ cup crushed pineapple
½ cup pineapple juice
3 drops pineapple extract
2 tablespoons rum
⅓ cup milk

½ cup whipping cream
Pineapple slices for decoration

Method:

1. Place gelatin in 4 tablespoons water and let soften for at least 10 minutes.
2. Drain the crushed pineapple, reserving ½ cup of the juice.
3. Beat tofu with an electric mixer or rotary beater until smooth. Rinse off the blades of the mixer so that they are clean for step 6.
4. In a sauce pan, heat the pineapple juice and sugar until the sugar dissolves. Add the softened gelatin. Stir constantly over low heat until the gelatin is completely dissolved. Do not allow to boil.
5. Remove from heat and stir in the puréed tofu. Add the pineapple extract and rum.
6. Place the milk in a bowl and add the tofu-gelatin mixture. With a clean electric mixer, beat until smooth. Let cool.
7. When the tofu-gelatin mixture just begins to set, whip the cream stiffly and fold in. Add the crushed pineapple, and mix gently. Pour into a mold which has been rinsed with cold water and chill in the refrigerator. Unmold onto a serving dish just before serving.
8. Decorate with pineapple slices.

Tofu Soufflé

A cheesecake-like dessert.

Ingredients:

4 eggs, separated
14½ oz. (410 g) sweetened condensed milk
Juice of 2 lemons
Grated rind of 1 lemon, or 3 drops of lemon extract
10 oz. (300 g) tofu, coarsely crumbled
2 tablespoons cornstarch

Method:

1. Preheat oven to 400°F. (200°C.). Butter a 1¼ quart (1.2 *l*) soufflé dish.
2. Beat the egg whites until very stiff, and set aside.
3. In a large mixing bowl, combine the sweetened, condensed milk, lemon juice and rind, tofu, cornstarch and egg yolks. Beat until smooth.
4. Fold in the egg whites, and mix lightly but thoroughly.
5. Fill the soufflé dish with the mixture and bake about 30 minutes or until set and browned on top. Serve immediately.

Hearty Pancake with Ham and Cabbage

Serves 2

Ingredients:
½ lb. (225 g) tofu, lightly pressed
3 oz. (100 g) sliced ham
1 oz. (30 g) cabbage (about ¼ cup, shredded)
1 egg
½ cup milk
1 teaspoon instant soup granules, or 1 cube, crumbled
3 tablespoons mayonnaise
1 cup flour, sifted
3 tablespoons vegetable oil
2 tablespoons minced parsley
Salt and pepper

Method:
1. Purée tofu in a blender.
2. Cut sliced ham into ½-inch (1 cm) squares. Shred cabbage finely.
3. Thoroughly mix together the egg, milk, mayonnaise, soup granules, and tofu.
4. Stir in the ham, cabbage, and flour. Season with salt and pepper. Heat a small frying pan. (A 7-inch (18 cm) pan is about the right size.) Coat with ½ tablespoon of the oil. Pour in half of the pancake batter, and spread it evenly over the pan. Cook over low heat. When the top begins to look slightly dry, sprinkle with half the parsley; then turn the pancake over and cook the other side. Repeat this procedure for the second pancake. You can also make both pancakes at one time on a griddle. Add extra flour, if necessary, so that the batter doesn't run too much.
5. Cut the pancakes into wedges and serve hot. A sauce made of equal parts of ketchup and Worcestershire sauce goes well with these pancakes.

Note:
The Japanese name for this pancake, *Okonomiyaki*, means "a dish made as you like it." Feel free to substitute other ingredients for the ham and cabbage; this dish gives you a thrifty and delicious way to use leftovers.

Glossary

BEEFSTEAK LEAVES: see *shiso.*

BONITO FLAKES: Bonito, a fish of the mackerel family, is filleted, then dried until it resembles a piece of wood. In flaked form, it can be purchased in packets for single use and in large bags. It is one of the basic ingredients in Japanese soup stock (see DASHI) and is also used to garnish tofu and vegetable dishes. In Japanese, dried bonito is called *katsuo-bushi;* the flakes are called *hana-gatsuo.*

CLOUD-EAR or WOOD-EAR MUSHROOMS (*kikurage*): Available dried in Asian grocery stores. Rinse clean, and soak in warm water until soft. Cloud-ear mushrooms are valued more for their crunchy texture than taste, which is rather bland; if unavailable, either omit or substitute any other kind of mushroom.

DAIKON: Giant white oriental radish, used grated or shredded as a garnish, and sliced in cooked dishes. Turnips are a good substitute, especially in cooked dishes; sometimes white icicle radishes and red radishes can also be used.

DASHI: Clear Japanese soup stock. There are 4 basic types, each with its own characteristic flavor:

KOMBU-DASHI: Use a 4-inch (10 cm) piece of *kombu* seaweed. Wipe with a damp cloth (do not wash, or you will lose much of the flavor), place in 4 cups of water, and let it sit for an hour. Heat to the boiling point, but remove the *kombu* just before the water actually boils.

KATSUO-DASHI: Heat 4 cups of water. Add 1 cup of bonito flakes just before the water reaches the boiling point. When the foam begins to rise, reduce heat and simmer for 10 seconds. Turn off the heat, and add a pinch of salt which will keep the water from absorbing more bonito flavor and becoming too strong. Let stand until the flakes sink to the bottom. Carefully skim off the clear liquid. For a very aromatic stock, combine these two types of *dashi.* First make *kombu-dashi.* After removing the *kombu,* reheat the stock, adding the bonito flakes just before it begins to boil. Proceed as above.

DASHI WITH DASHI-JAKO: *Dashi-jako* are very small dried fish which produce a stock with a strong fish flavor. This stock is used mostly for *miso-shiru (miso*-soup). Remove head and intestines of 12–15 *dashi-jako.* After washing them, let sit in 5 cups of water for 2–3 hours. Heat just until the water reaches body temperature. When in a hurry, soak *dashi-jako* in warm water for ½ hour, then heat just up to the boiling point—do not let the water actually boil. Strain.

SHIITAKE-DASHI: Use the liquid in which dried *shiitake* mushrooms have been soaked.

An instant *dashi,* called *dashi-no-moto,* is also available. Use 1 teaspoon *dashi-no-moto* to 1 cup water.

DASHI-KOBU: See *kombu.*

ENOKI DAKE: A white cultivated mushroom with a slender stalk and small cap. Since it is seldom available in fresh form, you can either omit it or substitute any kind of mushroom.

GINGER (*Shoga*): Fresh ginger root is used as a garnish and as a cooking spice. To obtain ginger juice, grate the peeled ginger and squeeze. Ginger shoots, which are called for in several recipes in this book, are a different variety of ginger. Fresh shoots are sometimes available in oriental markets in the spring; you can also find them preserved and pickled (*hajikami*). To make vinegared ginger (*sujoga*) slice a 2-inch (5 cm) piece ginger root very thinly, parboil, drain and marinate in sauce made of 1 tablespoon sugar, 3 tablespoons vinegar.

GINKGO NUTS: Seeds of the ginkgo tree. The tender, light-green nut lies inside several layers of casing. Canned ginkgo nuts are widely available in oriental markets.

KIKURAGE: See cloud-ear mushrooms.

KINOME: Young sprigs of *sansho,* a Japanese pepper tree. *Kinomé's* bright green color, pungent smell, and neat, symmetrical form express the freshness of early summer. Unfortunately, it is difficult to obtain *kinomé* in the West, so use a bit of celery leaves, water cress, or young spinach for a spot of decorative color.

KOMBU: Kelp or sea tangle. One of the basic ingredients in *dashi,* the Japanese soup stock. *Kombu* is packaged in various shapes and forms; for *dashi,* buy the long strips called *dashi-kombu.* (*Kombu* is also spelled *konbu* and *kobu.*)

MIRIN: Intensified, sweetened *sake.* Look for it in oriental markets, not in alcoholic beverage stores. As an alternative, you can use 1 teaspoon sugar and 1 tablespoon *sake* or sherry for 1 teaspoon *mirin.*

MISO: Fermented soybean paste. The colors range from yellow to brown; yellow *miso* is called "white" *miso,* and brown *miso* is called "red" *miso.* The degree of saltiness varies greatly. Refrigerated, *miso* stays fresh for many months, so you can buy several types with different flavors without worrying about spoilage.

MOMIJI-OROSHI: Grated *daikon* spiced with red peppers. Drill with a chopstick 3 to 4 holes lengthwise into a *daikon.* Insert dried chili peppers into the holes. *Daikon,* thus grated, has a slightly red color and hot spicy taste.

MITSUBA (trefoil): Long, thin stalks are topped with leaves deeply cut into 3 leaflets. A member of the parsley family, *mitsuba* is used in soups, *chawanmushi* (custard), and as a garnish. Young celery leaves, or a bit of spinach or watercress can be substituted for the color. Be careful not to purchase Chinese parsley (also called coriander leaves or cilantro.) It is easy to confuse the two for they are often placed next to each other in oriental markets. Chinese parsley has a very strong flavor and odor of its own and cannot be substituted for the delicate tasting *mitsuba.*

MYOGA: Pungent buds of a plant belonging to the ginger family. Available only in summer.

NAMEKO: Tiny brownish mushrooms with a slippery coating. Available in cans in oriental markets. You can substitute other kinds of mushrooms.

NORI: Often translated as "laver." A green to purple-black seaweed sold dried in paper-thin sheets. Store in an air-tight container. To improve its flavor and texture, before using it, toast by passing it several time over a gas flame.

SAKE: Rice wine. Purchase *sake* in an alcoholic beverage store. Sherry can be used as a substitute in an emergency, but *sake* is inexpensive and widely available, so try to have it on hand.

SEAWEED: See *kombu, nori, wakamé.*

SESAME OIL: Made from sesame seeds, this oil is used sparingly for seasoning dishes. It has a delicious, nutty taste.

SESAME SEEDS: Both black and white sesame seeds are used in Japanese cooking. The seeds are toasted and crushed in a mortar to bring out their characteristic flavor. Toast in a dry pan, shaking the pan and watching carefully; remove from the pan as soon as they become golden.

SHIITAKE: Black mushrooms which are popular in Japanese, Chinese, and Korean cooking. Sometimes available in fresh form, but usually you will be using dried ones. Soak in water before using. Cut off and discard the stems. Strain the water in which the *shiitake* were soaked and use as soup stock.

SHIMEJI: Gray-brown mushrooms with a small cap. Usually sold fresh. Substitute any kind of mushroom if you cannot find *shimeji.*

SHISO: A herb with brilliant green, fragrant leaves. (There is also a red variety used for pickling;

the recipes in this book call for only the green herb.) The English names for *shiso* are perilla (after the genus) and beefsteak plant; but they will be called *shiso* in most stores that carry the leaves. *Shiso* is cultivated in California; it also grows wild in many parts of the United States. Wait until the little flowers have gone to seed in the fall, pick them and plant them in the spring. A hardy annual, *shiso* is self-seeding; once you plant it, you will never be without this delicious herb. Besides being used to garnish dishes, *shiso* is deep fried in *tempura*. Possible substitutes as a garnish are fresh mint or basil.

SHRIMP, DRIED: A characteristic flavoring of many Chinese dishes. Dried shrimp must be soaked for at least 1 hour if being used in a simmered dish and even longer if being briefly stir-fried.

SOY SAUCE: Use Japanese soy for Japanese dishes; Chinese soy sauce is quite different. There are 2 types of Japanese soy sauce; *shoyu* (dark soy sauce) and *usukuchi-shoyu* (light soy sauce). Use *shoyu* unless otherwise specified. *Usukuchi-shoyu* is used whenever you do not want to darken the color of the ingredients in a dish; it tends to be saltier than the regular *shoyu*.

SZECHUAN PEPPER-SALT (*Hua-chiao-yen*): *Szechuan* peppercorns are reddish brown in color. Buy the seeded ones if possible; if not, pick through and discard the black kernels. Only the husks are used in cooking. The pepper-salt dip is a popular flavoring for deep-fried Chinese dishes. Combine 1 part peppercorns to 3 parts salt in a dry frying pan. Heat over very low heat until the pepper-corns smoke slightly. Cool and grind in a mortar or pepper grinder. You can also crush the peppercorns sufficiently with a rolling pin.

WAKAME: A seaweed which is sold either dried or salted. Dried *wakame* needs to be soaked in water and salted *wakame* rinsed thoroughly before being used.

WHITE RADISH: See *daikon*.

YUZU: Japanese citron. The fragrant rind is grated and added as a garnish to soups and other dishes. Not often available in the West, *yuzu* can be replaced with grated lemon or lime peel.

ZHA-CAI: A pickled Chinese vegetable resembling kohlrabi. You may also find it spelled "*cha tsoi*" or "*choan choy*." It is variously translated into English as pickled or preserved cabbage, mustard greens, kohlrabi, or winter vegetable. Refrigerate what you don't use in the recipes in this book; it will stay fresh for a long time. You can use it to add interesting flavor to Western soups and stews.

Index of Recipes

Italicized numbers designate illustrations

Recipes by:
Sumi Hatano (56), Kaoru Hashiguchi (34-37), Masahisa Hashiguchi (34-37), Hideko Higuchi (58), Yung-Ching Hshing (22, 38-42, 54), Sadako Kohno (18, 46, 48, 54, 60, 62, 64, 66, 68, 72), Junko Lampert (20, 76, 80, 82, 84, 87, 89, 90, 93), Fumiko Makita (50), Akiko Murakami (26-29, 49), Kimiko Ono (22, 74, 78, 80), Sawako Sakai (70), Michiko Sho (43-45), Isao Tsuji (62), Sue Usuda (52), Aiko Yamaguchi (30, 52), and Kazunari Yanagihara (Cover, 24, 32)